WILLMAKER ™

LEGAL GUIDE TO YOUR WILL

BY ATTORNEYS

BARBARA KATE REPA
STEPHEN ELIAS
RALPH WARNER

ILLUSTRATIONS BY MARI STEIN

Please Read This

We have done our best to give you useful and accurate information in this book. But please be aware that laws and procedures change constantly and are subject to differing interpretations. If you are confused by anything you read here, or if you need more information, check with an expert. Of necessity, neither the author nor the publisher of this book makes any guarantees regarding the outcome of the uses to which this material is put. The ultimate responsibility for making good decisions is yours.

NOLO PRESS   Berkeley, California 94710

Printing History

Nolo Press is committed to keeping its books up-to-date. Each new printing, whether or not it is called a new edition, has been revised to reflect the latest law changes. This book was printed and updated on the last date indicated below. You might wish to call Nolo Press (510) 549-1976 to check whether there has been a more recent printing or edition. New **Printing** means there have been some minor changes, but usually not enough so that people will need to trade in or discard an earlier printing of the same edition. Obviously, this is a judgment call and any change, no matter how minor, might affect you. New **Edition** means one or more major, or a number of minor, law changes since the previous edition.

Book design	Jackie Mancuso
Cover design	Toni Ihara
Illustrations	Mari Stein
Index	Sayre Van Young
Printing	Delta Lithograph

Nolo books are available at special discounts for bulk purchases for sales promotions, premiums, and fund-raising. For details contact: Special Sales Director, Nolo Press, 950 Parker Street, Berkeley, CA 94710.

First Edition (1.0)	September 1985
Second Edition (2.0)	April 1986
Second Printing	August 1986
Third Printing	October 1986
Fourth Printing	May 1987
Fifth Printing	November 1987
Third Edition (3.0)	April 1988
Second Printing	June 1988
Third Printing	March 1989
Fourth Printing	September 1989
Fifth Printing	December 1989
Fourth Edition (4.0)	August 1990
Second Printing	August 1991
Third Printing	April 1992
Fourth Printing	November 1992

Acknowledgment: *WillMaker* originated as a joint effort by Nolo Press and Legisoft to bring self-help law into the computer age. In 1992, Nolo and Legisoft parted ways, and Legisoft is no longer involved with this product. However, Nolo acknowledges the important and original contributions of Legisoft's Jeff Scargle and Bob Bergstrom.

ISBN 0-87337-146-1
Library of Congress Card Catalog No. 84-63151
© Copyright 1985, 1986, 1988 and 1990 by Nolo Press

WillMaker License

This is a software license agreement between Nolo Press and you as purchaser, for the use of the WillMaker program and accompanying manual. By using this program and manual, you indicate that you accept all terms of this agreement. If you do not agree to all the terms and conditions of this agreement, do not use the WillMaker program or manual, but return both to Nolo Press for a full refund.

Grant of License

In consideration of payment of the license fee, which is part of the price you paid for WillMaker, Nolo Press as licensor grants to you the right to use the enclosed program to produce wills for yourself and your immediate family, subject to the terms and restrictions set forth in this license agreement.

Copy, Use and Transfer Restrictions

The WillMaker manual and the program and its documentation are copyrighted. You may not give, sell or otherwise distribute copies of the program to third parties, except as provided in the U.S. Copyright Act. Under this license agreement, you may not use the program to prepare wills for commercial or nonprofit purposes, or use the program to prepare wills for people outside your immediate family.

Commercial Use of This Product

For information regarding commercial licensing of this product, (including use by educational institutions and nonprofit organizations) call Nolo Press during normal business hours at (510) 549-1976.

Disclaimer of Warranty and Limited Warranty

This program and accompanying manual are sold "AS IS," without any implied or express warranty as to their performance or to the results that may be obtained by using the program.

As to the original purchaser only, Nolo Press warrants that the magnetic disk on which the program is recorded shall be free from defects in material and workmanship in normal use and service. If a defect in this disk occurs, the disk may be returned to Nolo Press. We will replace the disk free of charge. In the event of a defect, your exclusive remedy is expressly limited to replacement of the disk as described above.

Your Responsibilities for Your Will

Although best efforts were devoted to making this material useful, accurate and up-to-date, please be aware that state laws and procedures change and may be interpreted differently. Also, we have no control over whether you carefully follow our instructions or properly understand the information in the WillMaker disk or manual.

Of necessity, therefore, Nolo Press does not make any guarantees about the use to which the software or manual are put, or the results of that use.

Any will you make using WillMaker is yours and it is your responsibility to be sure it reflects your intentions. Have your WillMaker will reviewed by an attorney in your state who specializes in wills and estate planning if you want a legal opinion about the effect of the will or become confused by any aspect of the willmaking process.

Term

The license is in effect until terminated. You may terminate it at any time by destroying the program together with all copies and modifications in any form.

Entire Agreement

By using the WillMaker program, you agree that this license is the complete and exclusive statement of the agreement between you and Nolo Press regarding WillMaker.

Apple Disclaimer of Warranty

APPLE COMPUTER, INC. (APPLE) MAKES NO WARRANTIES, EXPRESS OR IMPLIED, INCLUDING WITHOUT LIMITATION THE IMPLIED WARRANTIES OF MERCHANTABILITY AND FITNESS FOR A PARTICULAR PURPOSE, REGARDING THE APPLE SOFTWARE. APPLE DOES NOT WARRANT, GUARANTEE OR MAKE ANY REPRESENTATIONS REGARDING THE USE OR THE RESULTS OF THE USE OF THE APPLE SOFTWARE IN TERMS OF ITS CORRECTNESS, ACCURACY, RELIABILITY, CURRENTNESS OR OTHERWISE. THE ENTIRE RISK AS TO THE RESULTS AND PERFORMANCE OF THE APPLE SOFTWARE IS ASSUMED BY YOU. THE EXCLUSION OF IMPLIED WARRANTIES IS NOT PERMITTED BY SOME STATES. THE ABOVE EXCLUSION MAY NOT APPLY TO YOU.

IN NO EVENT WILL APPLE, ITS DIRECTORS, OFFICERS, EMPLOYEES OR AGENTS BE LIABLE TO YOU FOR ANY CONSEQUENTIAL, INCIDENTAL OR INDIRECT DAMAGES (INCLUDING DAMAGES FOR LOSS OF BUSINESS PROFITS, BUSINESS INTERRUPTION LOSS OF BUSINESS INFORMATION AND THE LIKE) ARISING OUT OF THE USE OR INABILITY TO USE THE APPLE SOFTWARE EVEN IF APPLE HAS BEEN ADVISED OF THE POSSIBILITY OF SUCH DAMAGES. BECAUSE SOME STATES DO NOT ALLOW THE EXLUSION OR LIMITATION OF LIABILITY FOR CONSEQUENTIAL OR INCIDENTAL DAMAGES, THE ABOVE LIMITATIONS MAY NOT APPLY TO YOU. APPLE'S LIABILITY TO YOU FOR THE ACTUAL DAMAGES FROM ANY CAUSE WHATSOEVER, AND REGARDLESS OF THE FORM OF THE ACTION (WHETHER IN CONTRACT, TORT, INCLUDING NEGLIGENCE, PRODUCT LIABILITY OR OTHERWISE), WILL BE LIMITED TO $50.

Contents

Users' Guide

1 About Wills

2 The Basics

3 About You

4 About Your Property

5 How to Leave Your Property

6 Structured Solutions for Simple Wills

7 Caring for Children and Their Property

8 Choosing a Personal Representative (Executor)

9 Planning to Pay Debts and Expenses

10 Making It Legal: Final Steps

11 Keeping Your Will Up-to-Date

12 Letters and Last Wishes

13 Estate Planning

14 If You Need Expert Help

Users' Guide

A. System Requirements

To run WillMaker 4.0, you need:

- an Apple Macintosh 512Ke, Plus, SE, or II-family
  computer with at least 1 meg of RAM (Random Access Memory)
- a printer (optional)
- Macintosh operating system version 4.1 or later (including System 7.0)
- one 800K floppy disk or hard drive

B. WillMaker 4.0 Package Contents

Your WillMaker 4.0 package should contain:

- one program disk
- a WillMaker manual
- a registration card

C. Making a Back-Up Copy

Make a copy of your WillMaker diskette before running it. Never use original software disks for anything other than making copies. Make a copy even if you are installing WillMaker onto a hard disk.

If you are already familiar with a particular copy process, use it to make your back up copy, then skip to Section F on Starting WillMaker.

The copying process is slightly different if you have one or two floppy disk drives.

1. If Your Computer Has One Disk Drive

- Insert a system disk, version 4.1 or later, into the drive. Turn the computer on.

- When the desktop appears, eject the disk by choosing Eject (⌘E) from the File menu.

- Insert the WillMaker disk into the disk drive. When the WillMaker icon appears on the desktop, eject the disk by choosing Eject (⌘E) from the File menu.

- Insert a blank, formatted disk into the disk drive. Wait until the icon for this disk appears on the desktop.

- Point, click and hold on the WillMaker icon. Drag the WillMaker icon to the icon of the blank formatted disk.

- You will have to swap diskettes back and forth into the disk drive to make the copy.

- When the copying procedure is complete, name the new disk WM working copy.

- Remove all diskettes.

- Label the copy and store the original diskette in a safe place.

- Use the copy as your working copy. Do not set the write protection tab on the disk; WillMaker will not work if you do.

- Go to Section F for instructions on Starting WillMaker.

2. If Your Computer Has Two Disk Drives

- Insert a system disk, version 4.1 or later, into the internal drive. Turn the computer on.

- Insert the WillMaker disk into the external disk drive. When the icon appears on the desktop, eject the disk by choosing Eject (⌘E) from the File menu.

- Insert a blank, formatted disk into the external disk drive.

If the disk you put in the external drive is not blank, all the information on it will be erased.

When the icon appears on the desktop, point, click and hold on the WillMaker icon. Drag that icon to the icon of the blank formatted disk.

- You will have to swap diskettes back and forth into the disk drive to make the copy.

- When the copying procedure is complete, name the new disk WM working copy.

- Remove all diskettes.

- Label the copy and store the original diskette in a safe place.

- Use the copy as your working copy. Do not set the write protection tab on the disk; WillMaker will not work if you do.

- Go to Section F for instructions on Starting WillMaker.

3. If Your Computer Has a Hard Drive with One Disk Drive

- Turn the computer on.

- When the desktop appears, place the WillMaker 4.0 disk into the disk drive. When the icon appears on the desktop, eject the disk by choosing Eject (⌘E) from the File menu.

- Place a blank, formatted disk into the disk drive.

 If the disk you put in the external drive is not blank, all the information on it will be erased.

When the Icon appears on the desktop, point, click and hold on the WillMaker icon.

- Drag the WillMaker icon to the icon of the blank formatted disk.

- You will have to swap diskettes back and forth into the disk drive to make the copy.

- When the copying procedure is complete, name the new disk WM working copy.

- Remove all diskettes.

- Label the copy and store the original diskette in a safe place.

- Use the copy as your working copy. Do not set the write protection tab on the disk; WillMaker will not work if you do.

- Go to Section F for instructions on Starting WillMaker.

4. Alternate Sequence if Your Computer Has a Hard Drive with One Disk Drive

- Turn the computer on.

- When the desktop appears, insert the WillMaker disk into the disk drive.

- When the WillMaker icon appears on the desktop, point, click and hold on the icon.

- Drag the WillMaker icon to the icon of your hard disk.

- Place a blank, formatted disk into the disk drive.

If the disk you put in the external drive is not blank, all the information on it will be erased.

- You will have to swap diskettes back and forth into the disk drive to make the copy.
- When the copying procedure is complete, name the new disk WM working copy. Remove all diskettes.
- Label the copy and store the original diskette in a safe place.
- Use the copy as your working copy. Do not set the write protection tab on the disk; WillMaker will not work if you do.
- Go to Section F for instructions on Starting WillMaker.

5. If Your Computer Has a Hard Drive with Two Disk Drives

- Turn the computer on.
- When the desktop appears, insert the WillMaker disk into the internal disk drive.
- Place a blank, formatted disk in the external disk drive.

 If the disk you put in the external drive is not blank, all the information on it will be erased.

- When the Icon appears on the desktop, point, click and hold on the WillMaker icon. Drag that icon to the icon of the blank formatted disk.
- You will be asked if you really want to replace the contents of the blank disk with the contents of WillMaker. Click OK or press the Return key.
- When the copying procedure is complete, name the new disk WM working copy.
- Remove all diskettes.
- Label the copy WM working copy and store the original diskette in a safe place.

- Use the copy as your working copy. Do not set the write protection tab on the disk; WillMaker will not work if you do.
- Locate the WillMaker folder on the hard disk.
- Point, click and hold on the WillMaker folder.
- Drag the folder to the Trash icon.
- Answer Yes to the dialog box asking if you want to throw away the applications in the folder WillMaker.
- Go to Section F for instructions on Starting WillMaker.

6. Alternate Sequence If Your Computer Has a Hard Drive and Either One or Two Disk Drives

- Turn the computer on.
- When the desktop appears, insert the WillMaker disk into the disk drive.
- When the icon for the WillMaker disk appears, point, click and drag the icon to the hard disk icon.
- A dialog box will alert you that the disks are of a different type and the contents of WillMaker 4.0 will be placed in a folder on the hard disk.
- Click the OK button or press the Return key.
- When the copy process is finished, drag the WillMaker disk icon to the Trash icon. Don't worry; this will not erase the disk, but will only cause it to be ejected.
- Insert a blank, formatted disk into the external disk drive.

 If the disk you put in the external drive is not blank, all the information on it will be erased.

- Make the hard disk window the active window by double-clicking on the hard disk icon.
- Locate the WillMaker folder on the hard disk; double-click on the folder to open it.

- From the File menu, choose Select All (⌘A). All the items will become highlighted.

- Point, click and hold on any of the items. Drag them to the image of the floppy diskette.

- When the copying procedure is complete, name the new disk WM working copy.

- Remove all diskettes.

- Label the copy WM working copy and store the original diskette in a safe place.

- Use the copy as your working copy. Do not set the write protection tab on the disk; WillMaker will not work if you do.

- Locate the WillMaker folder on the hard disk.

- Point, click and hold on the WillMaker folder.

- Drag the folder to the Trash icon.

- Answer Yes to the dialog box asking if you want to throw away the applications in the folder WillMaker.

- Go to Section F for instructions on Starting WillMaker.

D. Installing WillMaker 4.0 Onto a Hard Disk

You will need approximately 400K of space on your hard disk to install WillMaker 4.0.

- Start your computer and get to the desktop.
- Insert the copy of WillMaker into a disk drive.
- Point, click and hold on the WillMaker icon.
- Drag the WillMaker disk icon onto the hard disk icon.
- A dialog box will alert you that the disks are of different types and the contents of WillMaker will be placed in a folder on the hard disk.
- Click the OK button.
- After the copy process has ended, point, click and hold on the WillMaker disk icon.
- Drag the icon to the Trash icon. This will eject the WillMaker disk. Then store the disk in a safe place.

See Section F for instructions on starting WillMaker.

E. The README File

The WillMaker diskette includes a file named README that contains information and clarifications of problems that have developed after the manual was printed. To display the contents of this file on your screen, double-click on the README icon.

 Double-clicking on the icon will open the README file only if you have TeachText available. TeachText is supplied by Apple Computer on its system disks.

After TeachText loads, you can print the file by choosing Print from the File menu.

You can also print the README document by using the Print command from the File menu on the desktop. See your Macintosh User's Guide for more information.

F. Starting WillMaker

To start WillMaker 4.0, locate the instructions for the system you are using and follow the steps indicated below.

1. For Single Floppy Diskette Users

- Start your computer with a disk containing system 4.1 or later.
- Eject the system disk by choosing Eject (⌘E) from the File menu.
- Insert the WillMaker disk into the drive.
- Double-click on the WillMaker disk icon to open it.
- Double-click on the WillMaker icon.
- The program will start and you should see the opening screen.
- If the opening screen doesn't appear, consult Section H on Troubleshooting.
- If the opening screen appears, skip to Section K for instructions on using the program.

2. For Dual Floppy Diskette Users

- Start your computer with a disk containing system 4.1 or later.
- Insert the WillMaker disk into the second drive.
- Double-click on the WillMaker disk icon to open it.
- Double-click on the WillMaker icon.
- The program will start and you should see the opening screen.
- If the opening screen doesn't appear, consult Section H on Troubleshooting.
- If the opening screen appears, skip to Section K for instructions on using the program.

3. For Hard Disk Users

These instructions assume that you have copied all the WillMaker files into a folder on your hard disk. Consult Section D for instructions on how to do this.

- Start the computer and wait for the desktop to appear.
- Double-click on the WillMaker folder icon to open it.
- Double-click on the WillMaker icon.
- The program will start and you should see the opening screen.
- If the opening screen doesn't appear, consult Section H for Troubleshooting.
- If the opening screen appears, skip to Section K for instructions on using the program.

G. Making More Than One Will

The WillMaker program and its manual are copyrighted. The licensing agreement prohibits you from preparing wills for people outside your immediate family for commercial or nonprofit purposes.

To make a will for another person in your immediate family, including your spouse or domestic partner, children or parents, proceed according to the instructions here.

After you have made the will for one person, for example, John Smith, then either make another copy of the entire WillMaker diskette, or if working from a hard disk, copy the Will.dat file as follows:

- Select the Will.dat file.
- Choose Duplicate from the File menu.
- After duplicating, rename the copy of the Will.dat file to the name of the person whose will it is, for example: John Smith Will.dat.
- Restart WillMaker.
- From the File menu, choose Erase All and Start Over.
- Write a new will for the second person, for example, Mary Smith.

• When you are finished with the will for Mary Smith, copy the Will.dat file and name it: Mary Smith Will.dat.

Whenever you wish to revise a particular will, you must rename the individual's Will.dat file to simply Will.dat.

Example: Mary Smith Will.dat renamed to Will.dat

The Will.dat file is required to be available to the WillMaker program or the software cannot run. This file must be named Will.dat.

H. Troubleshooting

This section of the manual briefly discusses some of the more common technical difficulties you might encounter in running WillMaker on your Macintosh. Later in the manual, you will find help with how to enter information, guidance in making decisions, legal explanations and examples. Onscreen help is also available by opening the Options menu at the top of the screen and clicking on Help (⌘H).

1. Problems Reading the Diskette

If you insert the WillMaker disk and the following dialog box appears:

This disk is unreadable.

Do you want to Initialize it?

This means that your disk drive cannot read the disk—your disk drive is on the blink or is not a 800K floppy drive or the disk is defective.

Click on the Eject button or press the Return key.

Check the disk drive by using another diskette that you have used before. If the disk drive operates properly, then the diskette you have received may be defective. Contact Nolo Press Technical Support.

2. Additional Error Messages

Error	What It Means	What To Do
2	Address error	Reboot your computer and try again. If the problem is still there, disable any inits or reboot from another system and try again.
11	Miscellaneous hardware exception error. Accelerators return this error message when trying to run WillMaker.	Turn the accelerator off if possible and try running the program again.
25	Out of memory	If your computer has the required amount of RAM (1 meg), turn off all of your inits and try again.
27	File system map has been trashed	Reboot the computer, holding down the Option and Command keys until the dialog box comes up. Click Yes or press the Return key when asked if you want to rebuild the desktop. If the problem persists, reinstall the system from a locked system disk.
28	Stack has moved into application heap	Reboot the computer and try again. If the problem persists, reinstall the system from a locked system disk.
Freeze	If your machine froze but is working properly with other software, the problem is most likely the WillMaker disk.	Try running from a new backup or a new original. Also try rebooting without any inits.
Memory resident or inits	Some memory resident or memory-affecting utilities (such as multi-tasking environments) may be incompatible with the WillMaker program.	Try rebooting after removing any such utilities from your hard disk. Or, if you have two floppy drives, reboot with a different system disk that doesn't have the same inits.

Error	What It Means	What To Do
Mac printing problems	Most Mac printing problems are caused by the chooser being set incorrectly.	Select the Chooser from the Apple menu. Click on the printer type in the left-hand window. Click on the printer name or choose either the telephone or printer icon. Click on the Close box. Try printing again. If this procedure doesn't work, check your printer connections and try again.
Out of memory	This means that there is not enough memory available to run WillMaker.	If you are operating WillMaker on a computer that has the required 1 meg or more of RAM, first be sure you do not have any RAM resident programs in memory such as in a screensaver or print spooler. If you do, try disabling them, then rerun WillMaker.
Error 53	This means that a file is missing.	Compare the original with the working disk.
Error 53	This almost always occurs when working on a Macintosh with a hard disk and printing to an Apple laserprinter. The problem is in the System Folder on the hard disk.	Replace the file called Laser Prep with the file of the same name from the Printing Tools disk
Error 57	Communication between the computer and another device such as a printer or disk drive are being interrupted or incompatible.	Check all of the cables on your computer. If there are any hardware add-ons, disconnect them if possible. try rerunning the program.
Program cannot proceed	The disk is locked.	Unlock it by sliding back the write-protect tab.
Non-standard hardware	Any non-standard hardware attached to your machine such as co-processors, data acquisition equipment or accelerators which affects the operation of the computer's memory or processor may render your machine incompatible with WillMaker.	Run WillMaker with the suspect hardware disconnected if possible. Or run the program on another computer that does not have the extra hardware.

I. Calling Nolo Press Technical Support

If you have problems that are not cleared up in the Troubleshooting section, call Nolo Press Technical Support:

(510) 549-1976

between 9 am and 5 pm Pacific time

Monday through Friday.

When you call, try to be in front of the computer with which you are having the problem. And please have the following information ready:

Version of WillMaker (should be 4.0 or higher)

Type of computer (Plus, SE, II, etc.)

Version of Finder and System (which you can get by selecting About the Finder from the Apple menu while at the desktop)

Description of any special printer or monitor interface hardware

Any inits or control panel devices

Amount of RAM

The number and types of drives (floppy, hard disk)

The type of printer—if you are having trouble printing

The point in the program that the problem occurred

Whether you can duplicate the problem

J. WillMaker Information and Help

The WillMaker program and manual provide explanations of practical and legal aspects of each step in the process of completing your will. One of the most important features of WillMaker 4.0 is the onscreen help it provides. In the program, selecting Help (⌘H) from the Options menu will display information that will help you with the task you are performing, such as entering your children's names or deciding how to leave property to minors. To return to the main program, click the OK button or press the Return key.

Another helpful feature of WillMaker 4.0 shows the context in which the information you enter will appear in your will. This is to help answer questions such as: Should the names of my children be separated by commas? Should I enter the name of my county as the County of XXX or XXX County or just XXX?

K. Basic WillMaker Operations

1. Moving From One Screen to the Next

Click on the Next Screen Button

Some screens, including a number at the beginning of the program, do not request any input from you. But these screens give you important information. Simply read the screen and advance to the next screen by clicking on the Next Screen button or press the Return key.

On other screens, you must answer a question or enter some words before you can proceed to the next screen. As you do, you will then see your answer displayed in context—as it will appear in your will. If the answer is what you intend, click the OK button and you will proceed to the next screen.

If instead you wish to modify your answer, you can do so before going to the next screen.

2. Back Up to the Previous Screen

Click on the Previous Screen Button

Frequently, you may want to refer to information on a previous screen, or to change what you entered in answer to a question. To do this, click on the Previous Screen button, which will take you back one screen in the program. Click on the Previous Screen button once or several times to go back to the screen requesting the information you want to change. Each screen you back through will display your previous answer—with the answers on most screens appearing in context. You can back up this way at any point in the main sequence of screens in the program.

Once you have finished entering information, you need not back up, because you can go more directly and easily to any part of the program by using the Review and Modify screen you will encounter at the end of WillMaker. (See Section O4 for more information on the Review and Modify feature.)

3. Quit (⌘Q)

Select Quit from the File Menu

To quit the program, select Quit (⌘Q) from the File menu.

When you start up WillMaker again, you will return to the part of the program where you were when you selected Quit.

L. WillMaker Menus

WillMaker 4.0 has three menus: File, Edit and Options.

1. File Menu

Erase and Start Over

The Erase and Start Over option allows you to start afresh—without saving any of the information you have entered.

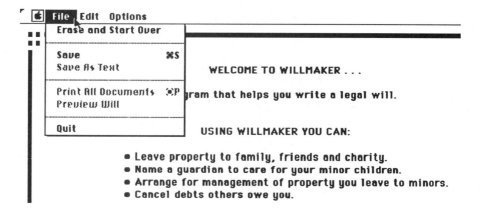

But first, the program will warn you that all your data will be erased. If you want to proceed, click OK or press the Return key and the information you have entered will be erased and the program will start over.

Save (⌘S)

The Save selection preserves your data and allows you to continue with the program.

Quit (⌘Q)

The Quit command will save your data and allows you to exit the WillMaker application. If you quit while in the middle of the WillMaker program and later resume your work, you will be returned to where you left off when you start up WillMaker again.

You can use the following commands only after you have entered all information required for a complete will.

Save As Text

The Save As Text selection creates a text file containing the will, self-proving affidavit, if an affidavit is available in your state, and the instruction pages.

Print All Documents (⌘P)

The Print All Documents selection will print your will, any affidavits and the instruction pages.

Preview Will

This selection displays the will on the screen so that you can review the information and the text of your will before you print it out.

2. Edit Menu

The Edit menu is similar to a wordprocessing menu for cutting and pasting
your answers to questions.

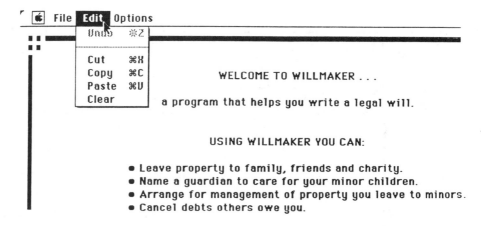

File	**Edit**	Options
	Undo	⌘Z
	Cut	⌘X
	Copy	⌘C
	Paste	⌘U
	Clear	

WELCOME TO WILLMAKER . . .

a program that helps you write a legal will.

USING WILLMAKER YOU CAN:

- Leave property to family, friends and charity.
- Name a guardian to care for your minor children.
- Arrange for management of property you leave to minors.
- Cancel debts others owe you.

Cut (⌘X)

The Cut feature removes the selected text from your document and places it
on the clipboard.

Copy (⌘C)

The Copy command makes a duplicate of the selected text and stores that
copy onto the clipboard, but does not cut it from the document.

Paste (⌘P)

The Paste command adds text that you have previously cut or copied into the
selected area.

Clear

This will delete the selection without putting it on the clipboard. That is, the selected text will not be saved.

3. Options Menu

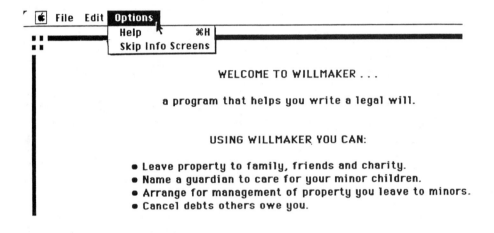

Help (⌘H)

The Help selection will display useful information about the legal consequences of making willmaking decisions. Help is available for each main screen in the WillMaker program. At any screen, you can select Help and information pertaining to that screen will be displayed.

Skip Information Screens

Some screens that appear in the WillMaker program do not ask you to respond to a question or provide information, but merely explain a particular aspect of making a will. You can turn these information screens off by highlighting them on the Options menu, and a checkmark will appear next to

Skip Info Screens. You will then be presented only with screens that require you to respond or enter data.

Because the information screens give you valuable guidance when preparing your will, you should skip them only if:

• you have used the program before and are thoroughly familiar with all of the relevant legal matters; or

• you are using one of the Structured Solutions in Chapter 6.

M. Answering Questions and Entering Information

1. Answers Requiring Choices

Yes/No Screens

Below is an example of an input screen that simply requires a yes or no response.

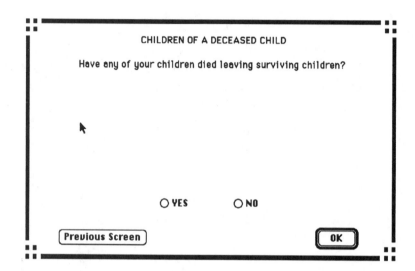

CHILDREN OF A DECEASED CHILD

Have any of your children died leaving surviving children?

○ YES   ○ NO

[Previous Screen]   [OK]

Click on the button next to the appropriate response.

If your initial answer is correct, verify that it is by clicking on the OK button or pressing the Return key. The program will then go to the next screen. If your initial answer is not correct—you accidentally hit the wrong key—click on the appropriate button; then click on the OK button or press the Return key.

Multiple Choices

Below is an example of an input screen that requires that you choose among
several options:

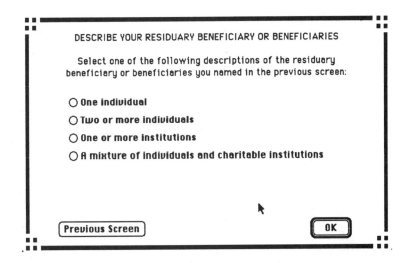

Click on the button next to your choice.

If your initial answer is correct, verify that it is by clicking on the OK
button or pressing the Return key and the program will then go to the next
screen. If your initial answer is not correct—you accidentally hit the wrong
key—click on the correct choice, then press the Return key.

2. Input Screens

Some screens in the WillMaker program require you to enter words—such as a name or descriptions of items of property. For example:

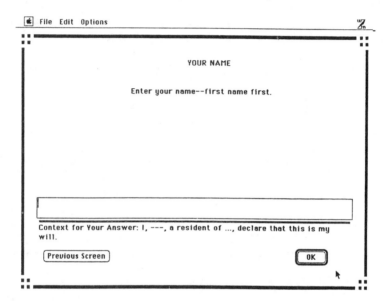

Below the input space, you will usually see a box containing a short fragment of text from the will—the context in which your current answer will appear when you finally print out your will. Use this as a guide to selecting the proper form in which to type your answer.

You can change your answer by correcting it within the input space if you wish to do so.

When you are satisfied with your answer, click on the OK button or press the Return key.

3. Lists: Bequests and Property Management

There are two parts of the program where you may describe one or more similar items:

1. Specific bequests You may make one to 28 separate bequests of specific personal or real property in your WillMaker will. Each specific bequest requires you to go through a succession of screens that will ask you to enter: the name of a first choice beneficiary, a description of the beneficiary (person, institution or both), a description of the property you are leaving to the beneficiary, directions for what should happen to the property if the primary beneficiary predeceases you and an optional alternate beneficiary.

2. Property management for minors and young adults For each of your specific bequests, you may have the choice of whether to set up property management—trusts or custodianships, depending on the laws of your state. To do so, you follow a series of screens to name a minor or young adult beneficiary, and then specify the name of the trustee or custodian, the age at which the arrangement terminates and an alternate trustee or custodian.

In both of these parts of the program, WillMaker displays a special screen of specific bequests and different property management arrangements. From this screen, you can do any one of these operations:

- Add a new item to the list
- Review or change the information contained in an existing item
- Delete an existing item from the list
- Exit the list by indicating you are done.

Example

Your first bequest is your jazz record collection to your nephew, Bernard. You would proceed through a sequence of screens in which you: name Bernard as beneficiary, indicate that Bernard is a single person and not an institution , describe the record collection, choose what should happen if Bernard does not survive you by 45 days and specify alternate beneficiaries.

When you are finished, you would see this screen:

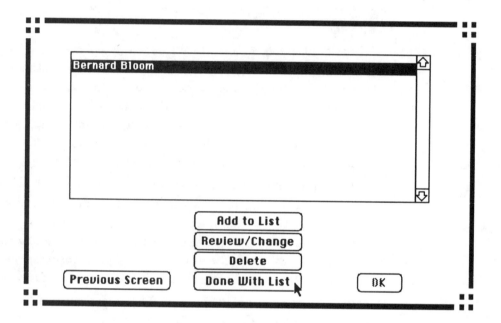

That is, you have completed one bequest, and the name of your first beneficiary, Bernard, is highlighted. If you want to make another bequest, click on Add to List to cycle through the questions again. You will be asked the name of this new beneficiary, and so on. If you do not wish to make any more bequests, click on Done with List. If you need to alter an existing bequest or property management, see Section N on Changing Your Answer.

Unfinished Bequest or Property Management

If you start a bequest—for example, you name a beneficiary, but you don't describe the bequest—you may inadvertently leave this bequest unfinished. This might happen if you back up to previous screens after naming a beneficiary, eventually reaching the screen that displays the list of bequests.

The potential problem is that, if you proceed with the rest of the program with only a partially completed bequest, the program could try to assemble your will with an invalid bequest. To protect against this, the program will warn you if you try to leave the bequest or property management list with an unfinished item. If you ignore the warning, the unfinished bequest or property management arrangement will simply be omitted when your will is printed, displayed, or made into a text file.

 If you quit in the middle of making a bequest or arranging for property management, when you next run the program it will return to the point you were when you quit. For this reason, it might be useful for you to make a note to yourself stating what you were doing when you quit, especially if you had to quit in the middle of a complicated part, such as the lists described above.

N. Changing Your Answer

There are a number of ways to change an answer you have entered. The simplest way is to use the Review and Modify option at the completion of your will (see page 41). This allows you to see your answer—and in some cases how it will be printed. If the answer is incorrect, you can change it.

For example, assume you have made four specific bequests so that the beneficiary list screen looks as follows:

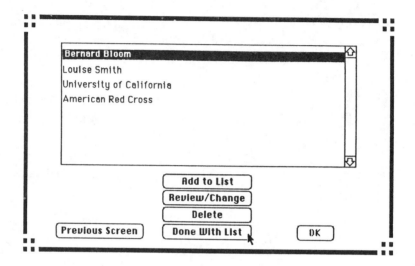

Now suppose you want to modify one of the bequests you have entered. Select the bequest and then click on Review/Change. You will be able to look at each screen and the answers you have entered for that specific bequest. Make the changes you want and you will be returned to the beneficiary list screen. Similarly, to delete a specific bequest, select the bequest and then click on Delete.

Changing a property management list works the same way.

Another way to change your answers is to return to them by clicking on Previous Screen. As you back up through the program, your answers will be displayed and you can change them. This is a slow and tedious way of changing your answers. Using the Review and Modify screen (see Section O4) is much faster.

O. Reviewing and Printing Your Will and Making a Text File

Once you have entered all the information necessary to make your will, a dialog box will be displayed that looks like:

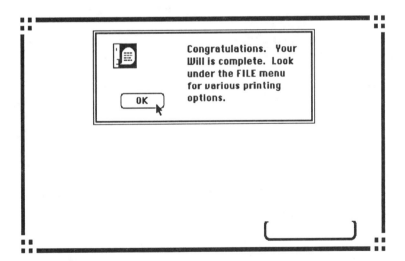

Congratulations. Your Will is complete. Look under the FILE menu for various printing options.

OK

When you are finished reading the box, click OK and the program will display the Review and Modify screen (See Section O4).

At this point, you can also view the will on the screen or print out the will by going to the File menu and selecting the appropriate response. It is a good idea to first review your will by clicking on Preview Will to display it on the screen as described below. This will allow you to look at the will without printing it out. You can read the will clauses, making sure that the information is correct. You can also get an idea of how the document will print out such as where the page breaks fall. After you have made sure the will is what you want, you can print it out.

1. Displaying Your Will on the Screen

To display your will on the screen, go to the File Menu and select Preview Will. You will then see a box informing you that the WillMaker program is assembling your document.

Wait for the program to assemble the will and display it on the screen. You can move around in the will by using the scroll bar, but you cannot do any editing.

To return to the main program from a displayed document, click on the Close box at the upper left-hand corner.

2. Printing Your Will

The final will documents include the will, the instruction pages and the affidavit, if available in your state.

WillMaker will handle the page breaks and margins automatically. The font used for printing is Times. In the print dialog box, entering page numbers in the From and To boxes will cause the program to print only the pages specified after the will and any affidavits that have been assembled.

After you have printed out the final documents, read Chapter 10 for information on how to sign your will and have it witnessed.

3. Making a Text File

A text file is a series of characters (letters, numbers, spaces) that is stored on a floppy diskette or hard disk. All word processors store information or documents in text files—and almost all such programs will be able to load the text file produced by WillMaker.

The most common reason to make a text file of your will is so that you can add special features (such as boldface type, large font size for the title) with your word processing program, and then print the will using the same program. **You should not change the language of your will under any circumstances.**

To make a text file, select Save as Text from the File menu. Then your will clauses will be assembled and saved. The text file will be saved as "Will of [your name]." To print out the will, you will have to open the text file with your word processor.

▶ Important Text File Notes

- Do not alter the language of your will.
- Each time you use the text file option, any text file you have previously made with the same name will be erased.
- To use a text file, you must use a word processing program to load the will text file using the Open feature of the word processing program. Consult your word processor's manual or the directions that follow if you are not sure how to do this.

How to Open the Text File in a Word Processor

If you are making a text file of your will with WillMaker 4.0, carefully read the information below about how to place the proper headers and footers to correctly format your will.

After you have made a text file and named it, start your word processing application. The steps for opening and editing the file are listed below for the following Macintosh word processors: MacWrite 5.0, MacWrite II, Microsoft Word, FullWrite and Write Now.

MacWrite 5.0

- Open MacWrite.
- Close the current document by clicking on the Close box in the upper left-hand corner.
- Go to the File menu; select Open (⌘O).
- Locate the will text file.
- Double-click on the will text file name.
- When the dialog box comes up, choose Paragraphs.
- When the next dialog box comes up, click OK or press the Return key.
- When the will document opens, read the instructions and important notes.
- Select the line:

    Page ____ Initials: ____, ____, ____, ____ Date: _____

    by clicking at the beginning of the line. Hold the mouse button down and drag to the end of the line.
- Go to the Edit menu and select Copy (⌘C).
- Go to the Format menu and open the Footer.
- Press the Return key once and then paste the Page and Initials line into the Footer by selecting Paste (⌘V) from the Edit menu.
- Take the # sign from the top left and place it in the page line at the spot where you want the page number to appear.
- Close the Footer.
- Locate the line of text that says Will of . . . .
- Select this line by clicking at the beginning of the line. Hold the mouse button down and drag to the end of the line.
- Go to the Edit menu and choose Copy (⌘C).
- Go to the Format menu; open the Header.
- Go to the Edit menu; choose Paste (⌘V).
- Click on the symbol for centered text.
- Press the Return key once after the "Will of ..." line.

- Close the Header window.
- Select the text for Important Notes, Instructions and Keep up to Date by clicking at the beginning of the line. Hold the mouse button down and drag it to the end of the Keep up to Date text.
- Go to File menu; choose Cut (⌘X).
- Go to the Edit menu and choose Select All (⌘A).
- Select the font and point size you prefer.
- Save the document.

   You are now ready to print.

MacWrite II

- Open MacWrite II.
- Go to the File menu and select Open (⌘O).
- Locate the will text file.
- Double-click on the will text file name.
- When the will document opens, read the instructions and important notes.
- Select the line:

   Page ___ Initials: ____, ____, ____, ____ Date: _____

by clicking at the beginning of the line. Hold the mouse button down and drag it to the end of the line.

- Go to the Edit menu and select Copy (⌘C).
- Go to the Format menu and open the Footer.
- Press the Return key once and then paste the Page and Initials line into the Footer by selecting Paste (⌘V) from the Format menu.
- Place the cursor at the position where you want the page number.
- Go to the Edit menu and select Insert Page Number.
- Close the Footer.
- Locate the line of text on the first page of the will that says Will of . . . .
- Select this line by clicking at the beginning of the line. Hold the mouse button down and drag it to the end of the line.
- Go to the Edit menu; choose Copy (⌘C).
- Go to the Format menu; open the Header.
- Go to the Edit menu; choose Paste (⌘V).
- Click on the symbol for centered text.
- Press the Return key once after the "Will of . . . line.
- Close the Header window.
- Select the text for Important Notes, Instructions and Keep up to Date by clicking at the beginning of the line. Hold the mouse button down and drag to the end of the Keep up to Date text.
- Go to the File menu and choose Cut (⌘X).
- Go to the Edit menu and choose Select All (⌘A).
- Select the font and point size you prefer.
- Save the document.

You are now ready to print.

Microsoft Word

- Open Microsoft Word.
- Go to the File menu and select Open (⌘O).
- Locate the will text file.
- Double-click on the name of the will text file.
- When the will document opens, read the instructions and important notes.
- Select the line:

    Page ___ Initials: ____, ____, ____, ____ Date: _____

    by clicking at the beginning of the line. Hold the mouse button down and drag it to the end of the line.
- Go to the Edit menu and choose Copy (⌘C).
- Go to the Document menu and select Open Footer.
- Press the Return key once and then paste the Page and Initials line into the Footer by selecting Paste (⌘V) from the Edit menu.
- Place the cursor at the position where you want the page number to appear and then click on the page # icon.
- Close the Footer.
- Locate the line of text on the first page of the will that says Will of . . . .
- Select this line by clicking at the beginning of the line. Hold the mouse button down and drag it to the end of the Keep up to Date text.
- Go to the Edit menu and choose Copy (⌘C).
- Go to the Document menu and select Open the Header.
- Go to the Edit menu and choose Paste (⌘V).
- Click on the symbol for centered text.
- Press the Return key once after the Will of . . . line.
- Close the Header window.
- Select the text for Important Notes, Instructions and Keep up to Date by clicking at the beginning of the line. Hold the mouse button down and drag it to the end of the Keep up to Date text.

- Go to the Edit menu; choose Cut (⌘X).
- Select the whole document by placing the cursor in the left margin; it will turn into a right-pointing arrow. Then hold the Command key down and click the mouse button.
- Set the desired font and point size.
- Save the document.

  You are now ready to print.

FullWrite

- Open FullWrite.
- Go to File menu and choose Open (⌘O).
- Locate the name of will text file.
- Double-click on the name of the will text file.
- When the dialog box appears, select Paragraphs.
- When the will document opens, read the instructions and important notes.
- Select the line:

  Page ____ Initials: ____, ____, ____, ____ Date: _____

  by clicking at the beginning of the line. Hold the mouse button down and drag it to the end of the Keep up to Date text.
- Go to the Edit menu and choose Copy (⌘C).
- Go to the Notes menu; choose New Footer.
- Go to Edit menu; choose Paste (⌘V).
- Click after the word Page.
- Go to the Edit menu; choose Variables. Select page number and click on Insert into Text.
- Close the Footer.
- Select the line of text on the first page of the will that says Will of . . . by clicking at the beginning of the line. Hold the mouse button down and drag it to the end of the line

- Go to the Notes menu and choose New Header.
- Go to the Edit menu; select Paste (⌘V).
- Close the Header.
- Select the text for Important Notes, Instructions and Keep up to Date by clicking at the beginning of the line. Hold the mouse button down and drag it to the end of the Keep up to Date text.
- Go to the File menu and choose Cut (⌘X).
- Select the remaining text and set the desired font and point size.
- Save the document.
  You are now ready to print.

WRITE NOW

- Open the translator.
- Choose Text to Write Now from the Convert menu.
- After conversion, quit the translator.
- Start Write Now; select Open (⌘O) from the File menu.
- Locate the will text file.
- Double-click on the name of the will text file.
- When the will document opens, read the instructions and important notes.
- Select the line:
  Page ____ Initials: ____, ____, ____, ____ Date: ____
  by clicking at the beginning of the line. Hold the mouse button down and drag it to the end of the line.
- Go to the Edit menu and choose Copy (⌘C).
- Go to the Format menu and choose Insert Footer.
- Choose Paste (⌘V) from the Edit menu.
- Close the Footer.
- Locate the line of text on the first page of the will that says Will of . . . .

- Select this line by clicking at the beginning of the line. Hold the mouse button down and drag it to the end of the line.
- Go to the Edit menu and choose Copy (⌘C).
- Go to the Format menu; select Open Header.
- Go to the Edit menu; choose Paste (⌘V).
- Click on the symbol for centered text.
- Press the Return key once after the Will of . . . line.
- Close the Header window.
- Select the text for Important Notes, Instructions and Keep up to Date by clicking at the beginning of the line. Hold the mouse button down and drag it to the end of the Keep up to Date text.
- Go to File menu and choose Cut (⌘X).
- Go to the Edit menu and choose Select All (⌘A).
- Set the margins by clicking on the ruler.
- Set the desired font and point size.
- Save the document.

You are now ready to print.

4. Review or Modify Your Answers

The Review and Modify screen looks like:

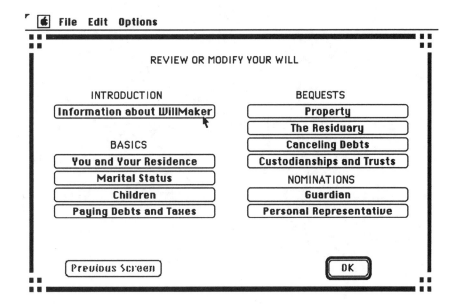

This screen displays the various parts of the program. To go back to a particular part of the program, click on the button corresponding to where you want to go. For example, to go back to the part of the program concerning where you live, click on You and Your Residence. The program will next display the screen where you entered your name. Your answer will be displayed in the context "I, John Smith, of California, San Francisco County, do hereby . . . ."

If you want to change an answer, the program will allow you to do so. After you have reviewed the section of the program, the program will return you to the Review and Modify menu—with one exception. If you have made a change in the information that affects other choices you have made in the program, the program will make you review all of your answers.

Use this menu to update your will whenever circumstances indicate you should. (See Chapter 11 for concerns about updating your will.)

Notes

Notes

Notes

Notes

Notes

Notes

Notes

Notes

Notes

Notes

1 About Wills

Making a will is an excellent way to ensure that your plans for leaving property to family and friends are carried out after you die. You can efficiently and safely write your own legal will using the WillMaker program. But before you start, it is a good idea to read this chapter and Chapter 2, which explain generally what a will can accomplish and how you can use WillMaker to meet your needs.

A. Making It Legal

For a will to be legally valid and to accomplish what you want it to, both you—the person making the will—and the will itself, must meet some technical requirements.

1. Who Can Make a Will

Most states require that a person must be at least 18 and of sound mind before he or she can make a valid will. (These requirements are discussed in more detail in Chapter 3.)

2. Will Requirements

The laws in each state control whether a will made there by a resident of the state is valid—and a will valid in the state where it is made is valid in all other states. Contrary to what many people believe, a will need not be notarized to be legally valid. (See Chapter 10, Section B for a discussion of notarizing self-proving affidavits.) The controlling laws put surprisingly few restrictions and requirements on the willmaking process. In most states, a will must:

- include at least one substantive provision—either giving away some property or naming a guardian to care for minor children who are left without parents;
- be signed and dated by the person making it;
- be witnessed by at least two other people who are not named to take property under the will; and
- be clearly written. No nonsensical language such as: "I hereby give, bequeath and devise" is necessary.

3. Handwritten Wills

In a minority of states, unwitnessed, handwritten wills (called holographic wills) are legally valid. And a few states accept the historical holdover of oral wills under very limited circumstances, such as when a mortally wounded soldier is uttering last wishes. But both of these approaches are fraught with possible legal problems. Most obviously, after your death it may be difficult to prove that your unwitnessed, handwritten document was in fact written by you and intended to be your will.

A properly signed, witnessed will is much less vulnerable to challenge by anyone claiming it was forged. If need be, witnesses can later testify in court that the person whose name is on the will is the same person who signed it, and that making the will was a voluntary and knowing act.

B. What Happens If You Die Without a Will

If you die without leaving a valid will, money and other property you own at death will be divided and distributed to others according to your state's "intestate succession" laws. These laws divide all property between a few close relatives according to a set formula, and completely exclude more distant relatives, friends and charities.

They are unlikely to mirror most people's wishes. Dividing property according to intestate succession laws is especially likely to be unsatisfactory if you are married and have no children, because most state laws require your spouse to share your property with your parents. And the situation is even worse for unmarried couples. No state's intestate succession law gives an unmarried partner any property.

Also, if you have minor children, another important reason to make a will is to name a personal guardian to care for them. This is an important concern of most parents who worry that their children will be left without a caretaker if both die or are unavailable. Intestate succession laws do not deal with this, leaving it up to the courts and social service agencies to find and appoint a guardian.

C. Basic Decisions about Property and Children

Making a will is not difficult, but it is undeniably a serious and sobering process. Before you begin, get organized and focus on a number of important considerations:

- What do you own?
- Who would you like to get your property?
- Who is the best person to care for your minor children and manage property you leave them?
- Who should you appoint to see that your property is properly distributed after your death?

This manual offers guidance on how to use WillMaker to implement your decisions in all of these areas. The choices, however, are up to you.

D. A Will Is Not the Only Way to Leave Property

Be aware that a will is not the only way—and in some cases, not the best way—to transfer ownership of your property to another person upon your death. Most property passed by will must go through a legal process known as probate, in which the will is filed with a court, property is located and gathered by an estate executor or administrator, debts and taxes still owed are paid and the remaining property is distributed as the will directs.

Probate has drawbacks. It can be lengthy, commonly taking a year or more. And it can also be expensive, often requiring the services of lawyers or other specialists. In many states, the lawyer handling the probate is paid a percentage of the total value of the "estate"—that is, the property owned by the deceased person at death. This fee arrangement typically means that a portion of your property you intended for family and friends goes instead to pay lawyers.

In short, if you are making a will—especially if you are older and have a large estate—consider whether it makes sense for you to plan now to pay the least amount in probate fees, and consider how best to use a will as part of a larger estate plan. (See Chapter 13 for an overview of basic estate planning techniques. For more in-depth explanations of estate planning techniques, see *Plan Your Estate with a Living Trust* by Denis Clifford, Nolo Press.)

Estate Tax Concerns Also, if non-tax-exempt property in your estate when you die is worth more than $600,000, the federal government will tax it. Your state may also impose inheritance and estate taxes on the property. Making tax-exempt gifts during your life, along with several other strategies, can reduce the size of your estate and by doing so, reduce its estate and inheritance tax liability. (See Chapter 13, Section D for an overview.)

Is a WillMaker Will Safe?

Traditionally, wills have been associated with rumpled-suited lawyers, quill pens and offices full of antiques—not with the high tech hum of computers. Times have changed. It is not easy to find a friendly, reasonably-priced family solicitor you can trust these days. Fortunately, the computer has quickly proven itself to be an ideal tool for assisting informed consumers in making simple wills. It will never betray your confidences or urge you to do anything you do not feel is right. And it won't charge you a cent to revise your will should your needs change.

The reason computers are such efficient willmaking tools is that writing wills involves little more than systematically collecting answers to well-defined questions, then translating the answers into tried and true legal language developed over hundreds of years. WillMaker, which has been in wide and successful use for several years, prompts you to answer the necessary questions— and produces a will that fits your circumstances and is legal in your state.

E. The Role of Lawyers in Making Wills

As a way to decide who gets your property, the will has been around in substantially the same form for about 500 years. For the first 450 years, self-help was the rule and lawyer assistance the exception. When this country was founded, or even during the Civil War, it was highly unusual to hire a lawyer to set out formally what should be done with a person's property. However, in the past 50 years, the legal profession has scored a public relations coup by convincing many people that writing a will without a lawyer is like doing your own brain surgery. This, of course, is nonsense.

What is true is that you may have a question about your particular situation that WillMaker does not answer. Or perhaps you
have a very large estate—worth over $1 million—and want to engage in some sophisticated tax planning. Or you may believe you would be comforted by having a lawyer give your WillMaker will a once-over. These are legitimate concerns and it is sensible to act on them. (Chapter 14 discusses the types of legal advice generally available and gives you an idea of how much you should expect to pay for it.)

F. Joint Wills—A Bad Idea

In the past, it was common for a married couple who had an agreed scheme for how to distribute all their property to write one document together: a joint will. But time has shown that idea to be fraught with difficulties.

WillMaker requires that each spouse make his or her own will, even if both agree about how their property is to be distributed. This limitation is not imposed to annoy people, but has good legal causes.

- Inevitably, one spouse owns some property that the other does not. Should even one of the two die without a will, the state will come in and claim this property, or distribute it to someone in the line of relatives. This is often contrary to what the deceased's wishes would have been had they been expressed in a will.

- Joint wills are intended to prevent the surviving spouse from changing his or her mind about what to do with the property after the first spouse dies. The practical effect is to tie up the property for years in title and probate determinations—often until long after the second spouse dies.

- There are also many court battles fought over whether the surviving spouse is legally entitled to revoke any part of the will.

For these and other reasons, joint wills have fallen out of favor. There are still some lawyers who will agree to write them for clients, but they do so in the face of the risk that such wills may become cumbersome or even found invalid in later court challenges. For these reasons, we strongly urge both spouses to write separate wills—a bit more time consuming, perhaps, but a lot safer from a legal standpoint.

2 The Basics

Because they reflect people's intentions of how and to whom they want to leave property, wills can be as complex and intricate as life. While laws broadly regulate the procedures for valid willmaking, you are generally free to write a will to meet your needs. Of course, this freedom can be dizzying to those who are not used to wading in the muck of legal documents.

Fortunately, WillMaker offers its users considerable guidance, so that the task of willmaking will be understandable and legal rules will not be trampled.

WillMaker's program works by having you systematically answer questions. Don't worry. As you will soon see, you either already have enough information to answer this easily, or you can quickly get your hands on it.

For Those with Basic Willmaking Needs

If you have very specific and simple willmaking needs—perhaps you just want to leave all your property to your spouse and name a guardian for your children, or divide your property equally among your children—it is not essential that you understand the many options offered by WillMaker. Chapter 6 contains simple step-by-step instructions that allow you to efficiently prepare wills in these and several other common and straightforward situations.

A. What You Can Do with WillMaker

This chapter gives you a quick survey of what you can and cannot do with the WillMaker program. Each area is discussed in greater detail, both in the program information screens and in other chapters in the manual. Using WillMaker, you can:

1. Name Beneficiaries to Get Specific Property

WillMaker allows you to make up to 28 separate gifts, called "specific bequests," of cash, personal property, or real estate to your spouse, children, grandchildren, or anyone else—including relatives, friends, business associates, charities or organizations.

Example
Using WillMaker, Robin leaves her interest in the family home to her spouse Lee, her valuable coin collection to one of her children, her boat to another child, her computer to a charity and $5,000 to her two aunts, in equal shares.

Example
Raymond, a lifelong bachelor, follows WillMaker's directions and leaves his house to his favorite charity. He divides his personal possessions among 15 different relatives and friends.

Example
Darryl and Floyd have lived together for several years. Darryl wants to leave Floyd all of his property, which includes his car, time-share ownership in a condominium, a savings account and miscellaneous personal belongings. He can use WillMaker to accomplish this.

2. Name Alternate Beneficiaries

Using WillMaker, all beneficiaries you name can inherit property under your will as long as they survive you by 45 days. The sole exception is for spouses, who need only survive you to take property under your will.

For every bequest you make using WillMaker, you can specify another beneficiary to take the bequest if your first choice dies before you do or does not survive by the required period. The reason that WillMaker imposes this 45-day rule is that you do not want to leave your property to a beneficiary—other than a spouse—who dies very shortly after you do, because that property will then be passed along to that person's inheritors. These beneficiaries are not likely to be the ones you would choose to receive your property.

Example

Gene wants to leave his house to his daughters, Jenny and Liza, in equal shares. Jenny has two very young children; Liza has two grown children. Gene wants to structure his will so that if Jenny does not survive him by 45 days, her share in the house will go to her husband Greg and if Liza does not survive him by 45 days, her share will go to her children. Using WillMaker, Gene makes two separate bequests—one to Jenny and one to Liza—of one-half interests in his house. He designates Liza's children as alternate beneficiaries for her bequest and designates Jenny's husband as an alternate beneficiary of her share.

3. Name Someone to Take All Property Remaining in Your Estate

All the property left over after you have made specific bequests of personal property and real estate is called your residuary estate. You can and should use WillMaker to designate a "residuary beneficiary" to inherit your residuary estate.

Example

Annie wants to make a number of small specific bequests to friends and charities, but to leave the bulk of her property to her friend Maureen. She accomplishes this by using the specific bequest screens to make the small gifts, and then names Maureen as residuary beneficiary. There is no need for her to list the property that goes to Maureen. The very nature of the residuary estate is that the residuary beneficiary—in this case, Maureen—gets everything that is left over after the specific bequests are distributed.

 If you want all your property to go to only one or to a small group of beneficiaries, you can make efficient use of WillMaker by skipping the specific bequest screens in the program and leaving all your property to one or more loved ones or a favorite charity by naming them as residuary beneficiaries. If you designate more than one residuary beneficiary, each will take an equal share unless you specify differently.

Example

Etta makes a will that simply names her three children, Ben, Ellie and Joe, as residuary beneficiaries. Since she has not identified specific property to go to these children, each child will get a third of her estate at her death.

4. Name a Guardian to Care for Your Children

You may use WillMaker to name a personal guardian to care for your minor children until they reach 18 in case there is no natural or adoptive parent to handle these duties. If your children need a guardian after your death, a court will formally review your choice. Your choice will normally be approved unless the person you name refuses to assume the responsibility, or the court becomes convinced that the best interests of your children would be better served if they were left in the care of someone else.

Example

Millicent names her friend Vera to serve as personal guardian in the event that her husband, Frank, dies at the same time she does or is otherwise unavailable to care for their three children. Millicent and Frank die together in an earthquake. The court appoints Vera as personal guardian for all three children since her ability to serve has not been questioned. If Frank had written a will naming another person to serve as guardian, however, the court would have to choose between those nominated.

5. Name Someone to Manage Property Left to Children

You may leave property to your own or other peoples' children. But at your death, property left to minors will have to be managed by an adult until they turn 18. And in many cases, it may be most prudent to have property left to them managed for a longer period.

WillMaker allows you to name a trusted person—or, if no one is available, you can name an institution such as a bank or trust company—to manage property left to a minor.[1] Management entails safeguarding and spending the property for the young person's education, health care and basic living needs, keeping good records of these expenditures and seeing that income taxes are paid. Management ends at the age you specify. What is left of the property is then distributed to the minor.

Do Not Use WillMaker for Beneficiaries with Special Needs

It is common to set up property management when a beneficiary is mentally or physically disadvantaged, or manages money poorly. The management provided under WillMaker is not sufficiently detailed to provide adequately for disadvantaged people, or those with special problems such as spendthrift tendencies or substance abuse. Management for people in these situations needs to be custom-tailored to fit their needs. If you need this type of management, consult an experienced attorney. (See Chapter 14 for guidance in finding and using attorneys.)

---

[1]The management methods available are different from state to state—and are discussed in detail in Chapter 7.

6. Name a Personal Representative or Executor to Handle Your Estate

With WillMaker, you can name a personal representative for your estate. This person, called an executor in some states, will be responsible for making sure the provisions in your will are carried out and your property distributed as your will directs. The personal representative can be any competent adult. Commonly, people name a spouse, a close, knowledgeable relative—or, for large estates or where no trusted person is able to serve—a financial institution such as a bank or savings and loan. Because of the risk of disagreement or conflict, WillMaker does not allow you to name two or more people to act as joint personal representatives. It is also wise to use WillMaker to name an alternate personal representative in case your first choice becomes unable or unwilling to serve.

Example
Rick and Phyllis both use WillMaker to complete wills naming each other as personal representative in case the other dies first. They both name Phyllis' father as an alternate personal representative to take their property in the event they die simultaneously.

Example
Rick and Phyllis do not wish to burden their relatives with having to take care of their fairly considerable estate. Each names the Third National Bank as personal representative after checking that their estate is large enough so that this bank will be willing to serve. They also investigate the bank's fee for this service, which is hefty.

7. Cancel Debts Others Owe You

You can use WillMaker to relieve any debtors who owe you money at your death of the responsibility of paying your survivors. All you need to do is specify the debts and the people who owe them. WillMaker will then include a statement in your will, canceling the debts. If a debt is canceled in this way, WillMaker also automatically wipes out any interest that has accrued on it as of the time of your death.

Example

Cynthia has lent $25,000 at 10% annual interest to her son George as a downpayment on a house. She uses WillMaker to cancel this debt. At her death, George need not pay her estate the remaining balance of the loan, or the interest accrued on it.

8. Designate How Debts, Expenses and Taxes Are to Be Paid

WillMaker allows you to designate a particular source of money or other specific assets from which your personal representative (executor) should pay your debts, expenses of probate and any estate and inheritance taxes.

Example

Brent owns a savings account, a portfolio of stocks and bonds, an R.V. and two cars. He uses WillMaker to make a will—leaving his R.V. and stocks and bonds to his nephew, his cars to his niece and his savings account to his favorite charity, Friends of the River. He also designates the savings account as the source of payment of his debts and expenses of probate. Under this arrangement, Friends of the River will receive whatever is left in the savings account after debts and expenses of probate have been paid.

Example

Calvin's estate is valued at over $600,000. It is probable that his estate will owe some federal estate taxes when he dies. He uses WillMaker to specify that any estate tax he owes should be paid proportionately from all the property subject to the tax. If there is estate tax liability, the personal representative he designates will require that each of Calvin's beneficiaries pay part of the tax in the same proportion their bequest bears to the value of Calvin's estate as a whole.

B. What You Cannot Do with WillMaker

WillMaker produces a simple will that meets the needs of most people. But there are some common sense restrictions built into the program. Some of the restrictions are designed to prevent you from writing in conditions that may not be legally valid. Others are intended to keep the program simple and easy to use.

1. You Cannot Leave Bequests with Conditions

As discussed, to ensure that property goes to people you want to have it, WillMaker automatically imposes the condition that, to inherit, each of your beneficiaries (except your spouse) must survive you by 45 days. But other than that, you cannot make a bequest that will take effect only if a certain condition comes true—such as "$5,000 to Ted if he stops smoking." Such conditional bequests are confusing and usually require someone to oversee and supervise the erstwhile inheritors to be sure the conditions are satisfied. If you doubt this, consider that someone would have to constantly check up on Ted to make sure he never took a puff.

So, to use WillMaker, you must decide whether or not to leave people property outright; you cannot make them jump through hoops or change their behavior to get it.

2. You Cannot Explain the Reasons for Leaving Your Property

Most of the time, the act of leaving property to people—or choosing not to—speaks for itself. Occasionally, however, a person making a will wants to explain why a certain bequest was made. This might be the case, for example, if you opt to leave one of your two children more than the other to equal out the loan you made during your lifetime to help one of them buy a house. Although the yearning to make such explanations is understandable, WillMaker does not allow you to do it in your will, because of the risk that you might add legally confusing language to the document.

Fortunately, there is an easy and legally safe way to provide your heirs with explanations for your bequests. Chapter 12, Section A of the manual shows you how to draft a letter that you can attach to your will, explaining your reasons for leaving property to some people—or not leaving it to others.

3. You Cannot Name Co-Guardians or Different Guardians for Your Minor Children

As discussed at length in Chapter 7, WillMaker allows you to name one personal guardian to care for all your minor children. At first glance, it may seem to be a good idea to divide up the job—naming two people or a married couple to agree to take on the responsibility of caring for your children if you die while they are still young. But a closer look reveals that naming co-guardians often presents more problems than it solves. For example, as life unwinds, the loving couple you named to jointly care for your children may divorce—making it impossible for them to be in the same room together, much less agree on the best way to raise a child. In such cases, courts are often called in to decide who is the most fitting guardian—a process that may be long, costly and very often heart-rending.

Also, WillMaker does not allow you to split up the job and name separate guardians for each of your children. That would render the program too complex for the rare occasions that such an arrangement might be useful. There is nothing surprising here. People who jointly own property or have children together should review their wills together to be sure they do not provide conflicting information—such as each parent naming a different guardian for the children in his or her will.

4. You Cannot Control Property Forever

Bequests given in a WillMaker will must take effect as soon as you die. You cannot make a bequest by will with the property to be used for a person's life and then be given to a second person when the first person dies.

Example

Emory wants his grandchildren to inherit his house, but wants his wife to first have the right to live in the house until her death. He cannot use WillMaker to accomplish this. Emory would have to leave his house in trust to his spouse for her life and then to his grandchildren upon his spouse's death. He should consult a lawyer to have the necessary trust prepared.

5. You Cannot Set Up Trusts to Avoid Taxes

If your estate is large—$600,000 or more—or if you are elderly or ill, tax-planning trusts may be important to preserving your property for your beneficiaries. WillMaker does not allow you to set up the types of trusts commonly used to lessen federal estate taxes, such as marital life estate trusts or generation-skipping trusts. To do this, you will probably need to consult a lawyer. (See Chapter 13, Section D, for more information on using trusts as part of your estate plan.)

6. You Cannot Require Bond of Your Executor or Property Managers

A bond is like an insurance policy that protects the beneficiaries in the unlikely event that the personal representative wrongfully spends or distributes estate property. Because the premium or fee that must be paid for a bond comes out of the estate, leaving less money for the beneficiaries, most wills for small or moderate estates do not require one. Following this general practice, the WillMaker will does not require a bond. Instead, you should take care to appoint someone you know to be trustworthy.

C. A Look at a WillMaker Will

You may wish now to take a look at a WillMaker will and instructions that print out with it. Do not be alarmed if the will does not exactly match the one you produce. WillMaker allows you to tailor your will to your property, circumstances and state.

WILL OF JAMES MOOREHEAD

I, James Moorehead, a resident of the State of California, Humbolt County, declare that this is my will. My Social Security Number is 544-674-9123.

FIRST: I revoke all wills and codicils that I have previously made.

SECOND: I am married to Janet Moorehead.

THIRD: I have the following children now living: Robert Moorehead and Alice Moorehead.

FOURTH: As used in this will, the term "specific bequest" refers to all specifically identified property, both real and personal, that I give to one or more beneficiaries in this will. The term "residuary estate" refers to the rest of my property not otherwise specifically disposed of by this will or in any other manner. The term "residuary bequest" refers to my residuary estate that I give to one or more beneficiaries in this will.

FIFTH: All personal property I give in this will through a specific or residuary bequest is given subject to any purchase-money security interest, and all real property I give in this will through a specific or residuary bequest is given subject to any deed of trust, mortgage, lien, assessment, or real property tax owed on the property. As used in this will, "purchase-money security interest" means any debt secured by collateral that was incurred for the purpose of purchasing that collateral. As used in this will, "non-purchase-money security interest" means any debt that is secured by collateral but which was not incurred for the purpose of purchasing that collateral.

SIXTH: When this will states that a beneficiary must survive me for the purpose of receiving a specific bequest or residuary bequest, he or she must survive me by 45 days, except that property left to my spouse shall pass free of this 45-day survivorship requirement.

SEVENTH: I hereby leave $1.00 to each of the following persons: Robert Moorehead and Alice Moorehead. These bequests are in addition to and not instead of any other specific bequest that this will makes to these persons.

EIGHTH: I give my residuary estate to Janet Moorehead. However, if the beneficiary named in this paragraph to receive my residuary estate fails to survive me, that beneficiary's living children shall take the residuary estate.

NINTH: Any specific bequest or residuary bequest made in this will to two or more beneficiaries shall be shared equally among them, unless unequal shares are specifically indicated.

TENTH: If any beneficiary under this will in any manner, directly or indirectly, contests or attacks this will or any of its provisions, any share or interest in my estate given to the contesting beneficiary under this will is revoked and shall be disposed of in the same manner as if that contesting beneficiary had failed to survive me and left no living children.

ELEVENTH: If my spouse and I should die simultaneously, or under such circumstances as to render it difficult or impossible to determine who predeceased the other, I shall be conclusively presumed to have survived my spouse for purposes of this will.

TWELFTH: If at my death there is no living person who is entitled by law to the custody of my minor child or children and who is available to assume such custody, I name Barbara Wilson as guardian of my minor child or children. I request that no bond be required of any guardian named in this section.

THIRTEENTH: All property left in this will to Robert Moorehead shall be given to George Wilson, to be held until Robert Moorehead reaches age 25, as custodian for Robert Moorehead under the California Uniform Transfers to Minors Act. If George Wilson cannot serve as custodian of property left to Robert Moorehead under this will, Barbara Wilson shall serve instead.

FOURTEENTH: I name Janet Moorehead as my personal representative (executor), to serve without bond. If this person or institution shall for any reason fail to qualify or cease to act as personal representative, I name George Wilson as personal representative (also to serve without bond), instead.

FIFTEENTH: I direct that my personal representative petition the court for an order to administer my estate under the provisions of the Independent Administration of Estates Act.

SIXTEENTH: Except for purchase-money security interests on personal property passed in this will, and deeds of trust, mortgages, liens, taxes and assessments on real property passed in this will, I instruct my personal representative to pay all debts and expenses, including non-purchase-money secured debts on personal property, owed by my estate as provided for by the laws of California.

SEVENTEENTH: I instruct my personal representative to pay all estate and inheritance taxes assessed against property in my estate or against my beneficiaries as provided for by the laws of California.

I, James Moorehead, the testator, sign my name to this instrument, this
_____ day of _____, _____. I hereby declare that I sign
and execute this instrument as my last will, that I sign it willingly, and that I
execute it as my free and voluntary act for the purposes therein expressed. I
declare that I am of the age of majority or otherwise legally empowered to
make a will, and under no constraint or undue influence.

_____

(Signed)

We, the witnesses, sign our names to this instrument, and do hereby
declare that the testator willingly signed and executed this instrument as the
testator's last will.

Each of us, in the presence of the testator, and in the presence of each
other, hereby sign this will as witness to the testator's signing.

To the best of our knowledge, the testator is of the age of majority or
otherwise legally empowered to make a will, is mentally competent, and
under no constraint or undue influence.

We declare under penalty of perjury, that the foregoing is true and correct,
this _____ day of _____, _____.

Witness #1: _____
Residing at: _____

Witness #2: _____
Residing at: _____

Witness #3: _____
Residing at: _____

Page 4

IMPORTANT NOTES

Before You Sign

Read your will carefully. Is everything printed as you intended? Do you understand the meaning of every word?

While You Sign

For your will to be valid you must be of sound mind and of the age specified by your state. This is almost always 18.

Your will must be witnessed by three witnesses, even though only two are legally required in many states. The witnesses should be in your and each other's presence when you sign the will. The witnesses need not read your will.

You must say to the witnesses that you intend this to be your will. Initial and date each page where indicated. Then sign the last page in the presence of the witnesses. Use exactly the form of your name printed on the will. The witnesses should state that they realize you intend this to be your will and they should then, in your presence, initial each page on the same line you did and sign the last page in the space indicated for witnesses, and include their addresses.

After You Sign

Keep your will in a safe place, where it can be readily found. You may make photocopies. However, only the signed original is legally valid and can be probated.

If there are major changes in your life, you should make, sign, and have witnessed a new will. Destroy the original of your old will and all copies. Changes that make it wise for you to make a new will include: having or adopting a child, moving to another state, the death of anyone named in your will, a change of marital status, and a significant change in the property you own.

Keep Up to Date

Fill out the WillMaker registration card in the manual and send it to Nolo Press at the address below. If you do not have a copy of the manual include $69.95 for a full WillMaker package.

3 About You

A. Who Can Make a Will

There are a few legal requirements that control who can make a valid will. Before you start your computer and get WillMaker going, make sure you qualify to make a will in the eyes of the law.

1. Age

To make a will, you must either be:

- at least 18 years old;[1] or

- living in a state that permits people under 18 to make a will if they are married, in the military, or otherwise considered legally "emancipated." Georgia law, for example, permits people as young as 14 to make their own wills if they are married.

2. Mental Competence

You must also be of sound mind to prepare a valid will. The usual legal requirements are that you must:

- know what a will is and what it does and that you are making one;

- understand the relationship between yourself and the people who would normally be provided for in your will, such as a spouse or children;

- understand the kind and quantity of property you own; and

- be able to decide how to distribute your belongings.

This threshold of mental competence is not hard to meet. Very few wills are successfully challenged based on the charge that the willmaker was mentally incompetent. It is not enough to show that the person was forgetful or absent-minded.

To have a probate court declare a will invalid usually requires proving that the maker was totally overtaken by the fraud or undue influence of another person—and that person then benefited from the wrongdoing by inheriting a large amount under the will. If the person making the will was very old, ill, senile or otherwise in poor mental condition when he or she made the will, it is obviously easier to convince a judge that undue influence occurred.

---

[1]Wyoming, however, is an exception. There, you must be at least 19 years old to make a will.

If a Contest Seems Possible

If you have any serious doubts about your ability to meet the legal requirements for making a will, or you believe your will is likely to be contested by another person for any reason, consult a lawyer.

B. Information Required by WillMaker

As you go through WillMaker, you will first be asked to answer a number of preliminary questions about yourself and where and how you live.

This chapter discusses those questions. The titles of the manual sections are the same as the titles of the screens in the WillMaker program.

1. Your Name

Enter your name in the same form that you use on other formal documents, such as your driver's license or bank accounts. This may or may not be the name that appears on your birth certificate. If you customarily use more than one name for business purposes, list all of them in your WillMaker answer, separated by "aka," which stands for "also known as."

There is room for you to list several names. But use your common sense. Your name is needed to identify you and all the property you own. Be sure to include all names in which you have held bank accounts, stocks, bonds, real estate or other property. But you need not list every embarrassing nickname from your childhood, or names you use for non-business purposes.

2. Your Social Security Number

WillMaker asks you to enter your nine-digit Social Security number. This is not a legal requirement, and you may choose not to provide it. However, it is a good idea to supply the information, because your Social Security number is often helpful to your personal representative and others who must track down your records and property after your death. This is especially true if you have a common name that may be easily confused with others.

3. Your State

Here you are asked to specify the state of your legal residence, sometimes called a "domicile." This is the state where you make your home now and for the indefinite future.

This information is important for a number of willmaking reasons, so it is important to doublecheck your answer for accuracy. Your state's laws affect: marital property ownership, property management options for young beneficiaries, how your will can be admitted into probate and whether your personal property and all your real estate located in the state will be subject to state inheritance tax.

If you divide up the year between two or more states and have business relationships in both, you may not be sure which state is your legal residence. To decide, choose the state where you are the most "rooted"— that is, the state in which you:

- are registered to vote;
- register your motor vehicles;

- own valuable property—especially property with a title document, such as a house or car;
- have checking, savings and other investment accounts; and
- maintain a business.

To avoid confusion, it is best to keep all or at least most of your roots in one state, if possible. For people with larger estates, ideally this should be in a state that does not levy an inheritance tax. (See Chapter 13, Section E, for a list of states that do not tax inheritance.)

If You Live Overseas

If you live overseas temporarily because you are in the Armed Services, your residence will be the Home of Record you declared to the military authorities. Normally, your Home of Record is the state you lived in before you received your assignment, where your parents or spouse live, or where you now have a permanent home. If this is still a close call between two states, consider the factors listed above for determining a legal residence, or get advice from the military legal authorities.

 ### If Your Choice is Not Clear

If you do not maintain continuous ties with a particular state, or if you have homes in both the U.S. and another country, see a lawyer to find out which state to list when using WillMaker.

If you live overseas for business or education, you probably still have ties with a particular state that would make it your legal residence. For example, if you were born in Wisconsin, lived there for many years, registered to vote there and receive mail there in care of your parents, who still live in Milwaukee, then Wisconsin is your legal residence for purposes of making a will.

4. Your County

Including your county in your will is optional, but recommended for convenience and as one additional way to help others identify you and to track down your property after your death.

Also, a county name may provide those handling your estate with important direction, because wills are probated through the court system of the county where you last resided, no matter where you died. The one exception is real estate: that property is probated in the court of the county in which it is located.

5. Your Marital Status

If you are married, see Chapter 4, Section C for a detailed discussion of property ownership laws affecting married people.

Here you list your marital status. For most people, this does not require much thought. But if you are unsure whether you are married or single according to law, it is important to clarify your status.

Some tips to help you:

- **Divorce decrees** Do not rely on word of mouth as evidence that you are legally divorced. Make sure you see a copy of the final order signed by a judge. To track down a divorce order, contact the court clerk in the county where you believe the divorce occurred. You will need to give the first and last names of you and your former spouse and make a good guess at what year the divorce became final. If you can't locate a final decree of divorce, it is safest to assume you are still married.

- **Out-of-country divorce decrees** It is often difficult to verify and evaluate the legality of a divorce that was supposed to have taken place outside the United States. If you have any reason to think that someone you consider to be a former spouse might claim to be married to you at your death because an out-of-country divorce was not legal, see a lawyer.

- **Common law marriages** It is uncommon to have a "common law marriage." In most states, common law marriage does not exist. But in some states—Alabama, Colorado, the District of Columbia, Florida, Georgia, Idaho, Iowa, Kansas, Montana, Ohio, Oklahoma, Pennsylvania, Rhode Island, South Carolina and Texas—couples can become legally married if they live together *and* either hold themselves out to the public as being married or actually intend to be married to one another. Once these conditions are met, the couple is legally married. And the marriage will still be valid even if they later move to a state that does not allow couples to form common law marriages there. There is no such thing as a common law divorce; no matter how your marriage begins, you must go through formal divorce proceedings to end it.

No matter what state you live in, if either you or the person you live with is still legally married to some other person, you cannot have a common law marriage.

- **Same sex marriages** No state legally recognizes marriages between people of the same sex—even where a religious ceremony has been performed.

The Importance of Your Marital Status

You should make a new will whenever your marital status changes. (See Chapter 11, Section A.)

For example, if you marry after making a will and do not provide for the new spouse, either in the will or through transfers outside the will, your spouse, in many states, may be entitled to claim up to half your property at your death.

Also, if you name a spouse in a will, then divorce or have the marriage annulled and die before making a new will, state laws will produce different, often unexpected results. In some states, the former spouse will automatically get nothing; in some states, the former spouse is entitled to take the property as set out in the will. And in a few states, courts will consider the entire will invalid.

If You Are Separated

Many married couples, contemplating divorce or reconciliation, live apart from one another, sometimes for several years. While this often feels like a murky limbo while you are living it, for willmaking purposes, your status is straightforward: You are legally married until a court issues a formal decree of divorce, signed by a judge. This is true even if you and your spouse are legally separated as declared in a legal document.

6. Your Spouse's Name

Enter your spouse's full name. As with your own name, list all names used for business purposes, following the tips suggested for entering your own name in Section 1, above.

4 About Your Property

This chapter discusses the grist of willmaking: what you own, how you own it and what legal rules affect how you can leave it. Once you have considered the information about property in this chapter, you will be ready to use WillMaker to leave it to others—a task discussed in detail in Chapter 5. Your children's rights to inherit property and your right to disinherit them are discussed in Chapter 7.

A. Your Property: An Overview

There are a few basic principles about property to keep in mind as you proceed through this chapter.

1. You Cannot Leave What You Do Not Own

You can only pass property to others if you own it. If you are married or own property jointly with others, you must be sure of what percentage you actually own and become familiar with the rules that may restrict what you can do with it. (See Sections B and C.)

> ▶ **Making Residuary Bequests:**
> ▶ **Your Beneficiaries Get Everything You Have**
> ▶ If you do not make specific bequests in your will but instead pass all your
> ▶ property through the residuary clause, there is less reason to be concerned about
> ▶ property ownership rules. All property you own at your death that is not passed in
> ▶ other ways will simply pass under the residuary clause of your will to whoever
> ▶ you name as residuary beneficiary.

2. Your Will Does Not Affect Property Passed by Another Method

In your will, you cannot leave property that you are passing by another method. The basic rule is this: Property in a living trust or a pay-on-death account (informal bank account trust), in joint tenancy or a retirement account or insurance policy where you have named the beneficiary, passes under the terms of that arrangement—not through your will. This is true even if you mention the property in your will. (These other ways to leave property are discussed in Chapter 13.)

Example

Laverne puts her house into joint tenancy with her daughter Linda. Later, she makes a will, leaving all of her property to her son Phillip. At Laverne's death, Linda gets the house.

The following property need not be included in your will:

- Real estate—also called real property—held in joint tenancy or tenancy by the entirety passes to the other joint owner or owners automatically.

- Joint checking, money market, brokerage or other financial accounts that are held in joint tenancy when you die also pass automatically to the surviving joint tenant.

- Life insurance and annuities automatically go to the person or institution you name as beneficiary, or if your first choice dies before you, the alternate beneficiary. You have no power to leave insurance money in your will unless you name your own estate as the beneficiary.

- Bank accounts and U.S. government securities which are held in your name with a direction to pay the balance to another person at your death. You can change this "pay-on-death" form of ownership while you are alive, but if you die with property owned in this way, the person you have designated will inherit it.

- Property you place in either a revocable or irrevocable trust passes automatically to the named beneficiary—not under the terms of your will. This includes property placed in a revocable living trust.

- Property left in personal retirement accounts, such as IRAs, Keoghs and 401K Plans. Such plans allow you to name a beneficiary and alternate beneficiary to take what remains of your account at your death. Once you do, you cannot change the beneficiary in your will.

3. Property Left By Will Goes through Probate

Probate is a court proceeding in which the authenticity of a will is established—and the deceased person's property is distributed to others. The probate process typically takes a year and often costs about 5% to 7% of the value of your estate in money paid to attorneys, appraisers and courts. The greater the value of the property passing through probate, the higher the fees. For this reason, many people choose to pass the ownership of at least their most valuable property to others through methods that do not involve probate—living trusts, joint tenancy, life insurance and pay-on-death accounts. (See Chapter 13, Section B for an overview of these estate planning devices.)

Probate, of course, does not present a problem until you die. For most people, that will be many years after they write their wills—and they are likely to rewrite their wills several times between now and then. Considering this, many people conclude that in mid-life, it is sensible to leave their property according to a simple will and also use that will to name someone to care for their children and a personal representative (executor) to wind up their affairs in the unlikely event of sudden death. More complicated estate planning, including taking steps to reduce taxes and avoid probate, is reserved until the property owner is older.

B. Forms of Property Ownership

▶ **A Roadmap to this Chapter**

If you are single and do not jointly own property with others, you need not worry about the material in this section or in Section C. Go on to the next chapter.

If you are married, do not own property with anyone other than your spouse, and you are leaving all or most of your property to your spouse, you also need not worry about ownership questions. Again, go directly to the next chapter.

If you are married, do not own property with anyone other than your spouse and your spouse willingly consents to a plan leaving a large part of your estate to others—perhaps children, charities or grandchildren—and you have your spouse's willing consent, you need not worry about the marital property ownership rules discussed here and can go directly to the next chapter. But make sure you and your spouse have a true meeting of the minds, because in most states your spouse can claim a 1/3 to 1/2 share of your property after your death if he or she asserts that claim. (This is discussed in Section C, below.)

 Also, in some states, a legal waiver must be completed and signed by you and your spouse. If you are in this situation, you may need to see a lawyer for this waiver before using WillMaker.

Depending on how you hold title to property, the law often imposes conditions on how you can dispose of it at your death. A look at some of the common forms of ownership and the legal repercussions of owning it in that form may be of help.

1. Owning Property Outright

The simplest form of ownership, of course, is when you are the only owner—that is, you do not share ownership and you are not married. This is called owning something outright. Of course it is possible that a lender has "legal ownership" in the property until you pay off the loan—as is true with car notes and mortgages. But for the purpose of making your will, you are the sole owner. Under WillMaker, the beneficiary of any property on which you owe money will inherit the property subject to the loan. This means the beneficiary of the property has the responsibility to pay off the debt.

2. Community Property

Community property is property belonging to married people in the eight states that recognize this form of ownership. (It is discussed in more detail in Section C1.) Generally, it includes all earnings and property acquired with those earnings during marriage.

3. Joint Tenancy with Right of Survivorship

Two or more people can own property—real estate or personal property such as securities or a bank account—in joint tenancy with right of survivorship. When one of them dies, his or her share automatically goes to the surviving owner, called a joint tenant. A joint tenant cannot use a will to leave his or her share of the property to someone else. But during life, joint tenancy is easy to change. Any joint tenant may end a joint tenancy by signing a new deed changing the way the property is held. The effect of this is to change the joint tenancy into a tenancy in common. Each person still owns the same proportional share, but because a tenancy in common does not include any automatic right of survivorship, each owner is then free to leave his or her share of the property by will.

Normally, joint tenancies with right of survivorship are created by language in the document (a deed, title document, or bank account certificate) that controls the form of shared ownership. To find out whether you own property in joint tenancy, see whether the document includes the words "joint tenants" or "joint tenancy." A few states require the document to read "joint tenancy with the right of survivorship," and Oregon, for example, requires the words "tenancy in common with the right of survivorship" to set up this kind of joint ownership.

▶ **States That Have Restricted or Abolished Joint Tenancy**
The following states have limited or abolished joint tenancy. If you live in one of these states and believe you may have a joint tenancy ownership, make sure you understand what it means. Pay special attention to the state rules about whether the joint tenancy property passes automatically at death.

Alaska	No joint tenancy in real estate, except for husband and wife.
North Carolina	No joint tenancy for any property except joint bank accounts.
Pennsylvania	No joint tenancy in real estate. Existing joint tenancy in real estate has been questioned in court decisions.
Tennessee	No joint tenancy for any property, except for husband and wife.
Texas	No joint tenancy in any property, unless there is a separate written agreement between joint owners.

4. Tenancy by the Entirety

This is basically the same as joint tenancy with right of survivorship discussed above, but is limited to married couples. When one spouse dies, the entire interest in the property then goes automatically to the other. Before tenancy by the entirety property can be changed to some other form of property ownership, both spouses must agree to the change. Nearly half the states now recognize tenancy by the entirety, but several of them—Alaska, Indiana, Kentucky, Michigan, New Jersey, New York, North Carolina, Oregon, Virginia and Wyoming—allow it only for real estate.

▶ **States with Tenancy by the Entirety Ownership**

Alaska	Maryland	Ohio
Arkansas	Massachusetts	Oklahoma
Delaware	Michigan	Oregon
District of Columbia	Mississippi	Pennsylvania
Florida	Missouri	Tennessee
Hawaii	New Jersey	Vermont
Indiana	New York	Virginia
Kentucky	North Carolina	Wyoming

5. Tenancy in Common

This is the most common way for unmarried people to own property together. In a tenancy in common, all owners have equal rights to use the property. Unless specified otherwise, ownership shares are equal, but it is possible to arrange for unequal shares by deed or written contract. Each co-owner is free to sell or give away his or her interest during life, and if not disposed of before that time, can transfer it to another at death under the terms of a will.

C. Special Property Ownership Rules for Married People

The great majority of married people simply leave all or most of their property to the surviving spouse at death. For them, the willmaking process is simple. The nuances of marital property law do not apply.

But if your plan for your property involves leaving it to many other people instead of or in addition to your spouse, the picture becomes more complicated. Questions of which spouse owns what property may then become important unless your spouse consents to your plan for property disposition, as is most often true when older spouses leave property directly to their children.

Under your state's laws, your spouse may own some property you believe you have the right to leave in your will. In some states, your spouse may have the right to inherit the family residence, or at least use it for his or her life. The Florida constitution, for example, gives a surviving spouse the deceased spouse's residence. And another legal rule states that even if you are the owner, your spouse may have the right to claim up to half of your property—whether you like it or not.

So if you are married—and this includes everyone who has not received a final decree of divorce—you should also become familiar with:

- the property ownership laws of the state in which you reside permanently, and
- the property ownership laws of any state in which you own real estate.

Fortunately, learning the basics of these rules is not difficult. States are broadly divided into two types for the purpose of deciding what is in your estate when you die: community property states and common law property states.

	Community Property States	Common Law States
	Arizona New Mexico	All other states
	California Texas	
	Idaho Washington	
	Nevada Wisconsin[1]	

1. Community Property States

In community property states, what you own and can leave by will consists of both your own separate property and one-half of the community property you and your spouse own together.

Obviously, then, if you live in a community property state and are making a will in which you plan to leave considerable property to someone other than your spouse, it is essential to learn what property you own separately and what is classified as community property. However, you need not be concerned about these property classifications if you plan to leave all or most of your property to your spouse—or your spouse supports your property disposition plans.

In community property states, a spouse's separate property is:

- all property the spouse owned prior to marriage, any property acquired by the spouse after legal separation, or property the spouse receives during marriage by gift[2] or inheritance, as long as it is kept separate from community property.

---

[1]While Wisconsin is not technically a community property state, it changed its marital property law on January 1, 1986 to resemble those found in community property states. This law covers all property owned at a person's death even though the property was accumulated before 1986.

[2]Community property can be transformed into separate property and vice-versa by means of gifts between spouses. Further, one spouse's separate property can be given to the other spouse as his or her separate property. The rules for how to do this differ from state to state.

Community property is:

- all employment income received by either spouse during marriage.[3] The one major exception to this rule is that all community property states except Washington allow spouses to treat income earned during marriage as separate property if they sign a written agreement to do so and then actually keep that income separate—as in separate bank accounts; and

- all property acquired with employment income received by either spouse during their marriage—but not after permanent separation; and

- all property that, despite originally being classified as separate property, is transformed into community property under state laws. This commonly occurs where either: one spouse makes a gift of separate property to the community, such as by putting a separately-owned home in community property ownership, or a spouse who owns separate property allows it to get so mixed together—or "commingled"—with community property that it's no longer possible to tell the difference between the two.

Example

John has $10,000 in the bank when he marries Elsie. This is his separate property. Over the next several years, John deposits a number of community property paychecks in this account and regularly withdraws money to pay bills—some of them for the couple's living expenses, some to pay for John's own optimistic habit of betting in favor of the Dallas Cowboys. The bank account balance fluctuates from a low of $2,000 to a high of $20,000. The separate property money in this account has been so commingled with community property that now the entire account is considered community property. John only owns half of the balance.

▶
▶
State Differences in Categorizing Property
▶
▶ The community property states have slightly different rules on what is classified as
▶ community property. One of the biggest differences is that in Idaho and Texas,
▶ income brought in by separate property is considered community property. In
▶ Arizona, California, Nevada, New Mexico and Washington, any income earned by
▶ separate property is also considered separate property.

---

[3]This generally only refers to the period when the two are living together as husband and wife. From the time spouses permanently separate, most community property states consider newly-acquired income and property as the separate property of the spouse receiving it.

Property that is Difficult to Categorize

Normally, classifying property as community or separate is easy enough, but in some situations, it can be a close call. There are several potential problem areas:

Businesses   Family businesses can create complications, especially if they were owned before marriage by one spouse and expanded during the marriage. The key is to figure out whether the increased value of the business is community or separate property. If you plan to leave your share of the business to your spouse, or in a way your spouse approves of, you have no practical problem. However, if you and your spouse do not have the same view of what is the best estate plan, it will probably be worthwhile to get professional help from a lawyer or accountant.

Money Judgment for Personal Injuries   Usually, personal injury awards won in a lawsuit are the separate property of the spouse receiving them. But not always. Whether such a court award is considered separate or community property can vary, especially if the injury is caused by the other spouse. In short, there is no easy way to characterize this type of property. If a significant amount of your property came from a personal injury settlement, research the specifics of your state's law or check with an expert. (See Chapter 14.)

Debts   Generally, either spouse's debts for food, shelter and other necessities of life are considered to be incurred on behalf of the marriage and must be paid from the couple's community property. Each spouse is individually responsible for paying personal debts. Unfortunately, the line between individual and community debts is not always a clear one. And, under some circumstances, one spouse's separate property may be used to satisfy debts for "common necessities" incurred by the other. Whether this is true depends on the law of each state, and may also be complicated by nuances of the circumstances.

Pensions   Generally, the proportion of pensions gained from earnings made during the marriage are considered to be community property. This is also true of military pensions. However, some federal pensions—such as Railroad Retirement benefits and Social Security retirement benefits—are not considered community property because federal law deems them to be the separate property of the employee earning them.

Examples of Community and Separate Property

The following examples can help you better understand how community property principles determine what you own.

Example
Ed and Babs are married and living in a community property state and have property consisting of:

- a computer inherited by Babs during marriage;
- a car purchased by Ed before marriage;
- a boat registered in Ed's name which was purchased during marriage with his income;
- a family home which Ed and Babs own together; and
- a loan[4] that Ed's brother owes Ed and Babs.

---

[4]Debts owed to you by others, such as accounts receivable, are a form of personal property and must be tallied up as part of your estate.

Property Ed owns and can leave using WillMaker consists of the car, one-half of the boat, one-half the equity in the family home and one-half of the debt owed by Ed's brother. The reasoning is that Ed's car was his before the marriage, so is his separate property; the boat and house were purchased with community property income (income earned during the marriage), and so Ed and Babs each own half-interests in them. The loan to Ed's brother was made from community property funds and belongs half to Ed and half to Babs. The computer, on the other hand, was inherited by Babs and so is her separate property. Ed can leave all his property in his will—and forgive one-half the debt.

Example

James and Sue Ellen are married. They live in Arizona, a community property state. They have $50,000 equity in a house (with a value of $150,000), which the deed specifies they own as "husband and wife," and a joint tenancy savings account containing $15,000. James owns a fishing cabin in Colorado worth $12,000, which he inherited from his father, and an Austin-Healy sports car worth approximately $10,000, which he purchased before he was married. In addition, James and Sue Ellen own $100,000 worth of stock in a blue chip corporation they purchased with savings from Sue Ellen's earnings during marriage.

Property owned by James and which he can leave in his WillMaker will includes:

- his one-half interest in the community property house (worth $25,000, or one-half of the equity);[5]
- his separate property fishing cabin;
- his separate property Austin-Healy; and
- one-half of the community property stock.

James should make no provision for his share of the joint tenancy savings account in his will, because full ownership of it will pass automatically to Sue Ellen if he dies before she does. And if she dies before he does, the property will pass as part of his residuary estate.

---

[5]James would also be wise to at least consider the several common techniques for transferring valuable property to others outside of a will, and thus outside of probate. It is often particularly advisable to do this with mortgaged real property, because if the property is left by will, in some states including California, the entire value of the deceased person's property—in this case, half of $150,000, or $75,000—will be counted when computing probate fees.

2. Common Law Property States

Common law property states are all states other than Arizona, California, Idaho, Mississippi, Nevada, New Mexico, Texas, Washington and Wisconsin.

In common law property states, the property you own consists of:

- all property you purchased with your separate property or separate income, *and*

- property you own separately in your name if it has a title slip, deed or other legal ownership document.

In common law states, the key to ownership for many types of valuable property is whose name is on the title. If you earn or inherit money to buy a house, and title is taken in both your name and your spouse's, you both own the house. If your spouse earns the money, but you take title in your name alone, you own it. If the property is valuable, but has no title document, such as a computer, then the person whose income or property is used to pay for it owns it. If joint income is used, then ownership is joint—generally considered to be a tenancy in common, unless a written agreement provides for a joint tenancy or a tenancy by the entirety.

Example

Will and Jane are married and live in Kentucky, a common law property state. They have five children. Shortly after their marriage, Jane wrote an extremely popular computer program that helps doctors diagnose a variety of ills. Jane has received royalties averaging about $200,000 a year over a ten-year period. Jane has used the royalties to buy a car, yacht and mountain cabin—all registered in her name alone. The couple also owns a house as joint tenants. In addition, Jane owns a number of family heirlooms which she inherited from her parents. Throughout their marriage, Jane and Will have maintained separate savings accounts. Will works as a computer engineer and has deposited all of his income into his account. The balance of Jane's royalties has been placed in her account, which now contains $75,000.

Property owned by Jane alone consists of:

- the car, yacht and cabin, since there are title documents listing the property in her name. If there were no such documents, she would still own them because they were purchased with her income;

- the savings account that is listed in her name alone;

- the family heirlooms; and
- one-half of the interest in the house.[6]

Example

Martha and Scott, who are married, have both worked for 30 years as schoolteachers in Michigan, a common law state. Generally, Scott and Martha pooled their income and jointly purchased a house, worth $200,000 (in both their names as joint tenants), cars (one in Martha's name, worth $5,000 and one in Scott's, worth $3,000), a share in a vacation condominium, worth $23,000 (in both names as joint tenants), and household furniture. Each maintains a separate savings account (approximately $15,000 in each), and they also have a joint tenancy checking account containing $2,000. In addition, Scott and his sister own a piece of land as tenants in common.

Property owned by Scott and which he can leave by will includes: his car, savings account, one-half the land he owns with his sister and half the furniture. Martha owns her car, her savings account and half the furniture and can use WillMaker to leave it. Scott and Martha jointly own the house and condo, but unless they take this property out of joint tenancy, the survivor automatically gets both and neither one can pass the property in his or her will.

Your Spouse Is Entitled to a Share of Your Property

Despite property ownership rules, if you intend to leave your spouse very little or no property, you may run into some legal roadblocks. All common law property states protect a surviving spouse from being completely disinherited—and most assure that a spouse has the right to receive a substantial share of a deceased spouse's property.[7]

---

[6]Although the half-interest in house is in Jane's estate, it would go to Will outside of the probate estate because of its joint tenancy status. However, if the house was in Jane's name alone, it would be her property, even if purchased with money she earned during the marriage, or even if purchased with Will's money.

[7]Some states in both categories (common law and community property) provide additional, relatively minor protection devices such as "family allowances" and "probate homesteads." These vary from state to state in too much detail to discuss here. Generally, however, these devices attempt to assure that your spouse and children are not totally left out in the cold after your death, by allowing them temporary protection, such as the right to remain in the family home for a short period, or funds—typically, while an estate is being probated. Accordingly, they should not prove unwelcome to any of you.

A shortchanged surviving spouse usually has the option of either taking what the will provides (called "taking under the will") or rejecting the gift and instead taking the minimum share allowed by state law (called "taking against the will"). Of course, these are just options; a spouse who is not unhappy with the share he or she receives by will is free to let it stand.

Laws protecting spouses are similar, but are not exactly alike in any two states. In most common law property states, a spouse is entitled to one-third of the property left in the will. In a few, it is one-half. The exact amount of the spouse's minimum share often depends on whether there are also minor children and whether the spouse has been provided for outside the will by trusts or other means.

Example

Leonard's will gives $50,000 to his second wife, June, and leaves the rest of his property, totaling $400,000, to be divided between May and April, his daughters from his first marriage. June can choose instead to receive her statutory share of Leonard's estate, which will be far more than $50,000. To the probable dismay of May and April, their shares will be substantially reduced; they will split what is left of Leonard's property after June gets her statutory share.

How a Spouse's Share Is Calculated

In many common law states, the property share that the surviving spouse is entitled to receive is measured both by what that spouse receives under the will and outside of the will by transfer devices such as joint tenancy and living trusts. The total of both of these is called the "augmented" estate.

While the augmented estate concept is rather complicated, its purpose is easy to grasp. Basically, all property of a deceased spouse, not just the property left by will, is taken into account in determining whether a spouse has been left at least the minimum statutory share. In determining whether a surviving spouse has been provided for adequately, the probate court will compute the value of the property the spouse has received outside of probate, and will also count the value of the property that passes through probate. This makes sense because many people devise ways to pass their property to others outside of wills to avoid probate fees.

Example

Alice leaves $10,000 to her husband, Mike, and $7,000 to each of her three daughters in her will. However, by a living trust, Alice also leaves Mike real estate worth $500,000. The total Mike receives from the augmented estate, $510,000, is more than one-half of Alice's total property, so he would have nothing to gain by exercising his option of ignoring the will and taking his statutory share instead.

▶ Moving from State to State

Complications may set in when a husband and wife acquire property in a non-community property state and then move to a community property state. California and Idaho treat the earlier-acquired property just as if it had been acquired in the community property state. The legal jargon for this type of property is "quasi-community property."

The other community property states do not recognize the quasi-community property concept for willmaking purposes, and instead go by the rules of the state where the property was acquired. Thus, if you and your spouse move from a non-community property state into California or Idaho, all of your property is treated according to community property rules. However, if you move to any of the other community property states from a common law state, you must assess your property according to the rules of the state where the property was acquired.

Couples who move from a community property state to a common law state face the opposite problem. Generally, each spouse retains one-half interest in the community property the couple accumulated while living in the community property state. However, if there is a conflict after your death, it can get messy; the reasoning of the courts in dealing with the problem has not been consistent.

If You Move

If you have moved from a community property state to a common law state, and you and your spouse have any disagreement as to who owns what, you will need to check with a lawyer.

The following chart provides a cursory outline of the basic rights that states give to the surviving spouse. It does not set out the specifics of every state's law, as the laws in many states are quite complex in this area.

Spouse's Share in Common Law States

1. **Surviving spouse receives right to use one-third of the deceased spouse's real property for the rest of his or her life**

Connecticut	Rhode Island	Virginia
Kentucky	South Carolina	West Virginia
Ohio	Vermont	

2. **Surviving spouse receives percentage of estate**

   a. Fixed percentage

Alabama	1/3 of augmented estate
Alaska	1/3 of augmented estate
Colorado	1/2 of augmented estate
Delaware	1/3 of estate
District of Columbia	1/2 of estate
Florida	30% of estate
Hawaii	1/3 of estate
Iowa	1/3 of estate
Maine	1/3 of augmented estate
Minnesota	1/3 of augmented estate
Montana	1/3 of augmented estate
Nebraska	1/2 of augmented estate
New Jersey	1/3 of augmented estate
North Dakota	1/3 of augmented estate
Oregon	1/4 of estate
Pennsylvania	1/3 of estate
South Dakota	1/3 of augmented estate
Tennessee	1/3 of estate
Utah	1/3 of augmented estate

   b Percentage varies if there are children (usually one-half if no children, one-third if children)

Arkansas	Michigan	North Carolina
Illinois	Mississippi	Ohio
Indiana	Missouri	Oklahoma
Kansas	New Hampshire	Virginia
Maryland	New York	Wyoming
Massachusetts		

Leaving Little to a Spouse

If you do not plan to transfer at least one-half of your property to your spouse in your will and have not provided for him or her generously outside your will, consult with a lawyer.

5 How to Leave Your Property

People who have worked hard to accumulate a fair amount of property understandably want to decide who it goes to after they die. Accomplishing this as efficiently as possible is what using a WillMaker will is all about.

WillMaker uses two approaches to passing property:

- You can make specific bequests in which you name specific beneficiaries to get specific property. As part of every specific bequest, you have the option of naming an alternate beneficiary in case your first choice does not survive you. If you wish to make one or more specific bequests, the program leads you step-by-step through that process—up to 28 times.

- You can designate a residuary beneficiary to take your residuary estate—all property you have not passed either in a specific bequest or by some other legal method. You can also name an alternate residuary beneficiary who will inherit if your first choice fails to survive you. If you wish to leave your entire estate to one or a few beneficiaries, you may skip the specific bequests entirely and just leave all your property in the form of one residuary bequest.

Easy and Quick Willmaking Solutions

If you are on the brink of a trip or otherwise pressed for time and need to make a will quickly as an interim measure—or have a simple plan for how and to whom you wish to leave property—see Chapter 6, Structured Solutions for Simple Wills. That chapter guides you, step-by-step, keystroke-by-keystroke through the willmaking process to help you make a simple, legal will efficiently.

A. Specific Bequests

A specific bequest is a gift of named property—for example, a house, cash, an heirloom, a car—to one or more individuals or charitable institutions that you designate. WillMaker lets you make up to 28 specific bequests.

For each specific bequest, you encounter screens that ask you to:

- name one or more beneficiaries;

- identify the number of beneficiaries and whether they are people or institutions;
- describe the property being left;
- describe what happens to the property if one or more beneficiaries fails to survive you; and
- identify one or more alternate beneficiaries.

For specific bequests to charitable institutions, you will encounter only the first three of these screens—since it is presumed that the institution will survive you.

The number of items you may leave in each specific bequest is limited only by the space available in the program for describing them. For example, "my silver engraved watch, antique gold locket and watchslide bracelet to Lucy Morant" qualifies as one specific bequest to Lucy.

Because it makes sense to group similar items of property left to one beneficiary—"all my clothing," "my woodworking tools," "my carrier pigeons"—there should be plenty of room for you to include all the property you wish to in each specific bequest.

1. Property Not Covered by Your Will

The first information screen in the specific bequest part of the program describes property that should not be left in your will. (Chapter 4, Section A, contains a more detailed list.)

If you have already arranged to leave property outside your will by using legal devices such as life insurance, pay-on-death bank accounts or living trusts, you do not need to include that property in your will. Some people worry that one of these alternative forms of property disposition might fail to do the job for some reason, and want to include it as a specific bequest just in case that happens. There is no need to do this. As long as you use WillMaker to name a residuary beneficiary, the property will have a place to go. The person named to take your residuary estate will be entitled to all property you do not dispose of in some other way. (See Section H, below, for a detailed discussion of the residuary estate and how it functions.)

2. Don't Place Conditions on Bequests

The next WillMaker screen warns against placing conditions on bequests. Sometimes this sort of bequest is illegal. Often, placing conditions on gifts risks making a confusing and even unenforceable will.

▸ A Beneficiary Must Survive 45 Days to Inherit

WillMaker automatically puts one condition in your will; a beneficiary must survive you by 45 days. Only bequests to spouses are exempt from this 45-day survivorship period.

This survivorship condition is essential because 45 days is the minimum amount of time it usually takes to turn property over to beneficiaries. In reality, the timespan is longer. WillMaker assumes that if a beneficiary only survives you by a few days or weeks, you would prefer the property to pass to an alternate or residuary beneficiary named in your will.

Other than this one exception, WillMaker does not allow you to leave bequests that depend on the beneficiaries meeting some condition you place on them or on the property. For example, you are not allowed to leave: "My gold Rolex to Andres, but only if he divorces his current wife, Samantha." The law will not consider such a gift valid, since it actually encourages the break-up of a family.

Another unacceptable gift would be: "My dental office equipment to my nephew, Claude, as long as he sets up a dental practice in San Francisco." The reason this bequest is unwieldy becomes more obvious once you think ahead to the need for constant supervision. Who would be responsible for tracking Claude's dentistry career and making sure he ends up in San Francisco? What if Claude initially practices orthodontia in San Francisco, using the equipment he was willed, then moves north to grow wine grapes in the Napa Valley? Must he give the equipment back? To whom?

WillMaker also asks you not to place conditions on the property you give in your will to others, such as: "My vintage Barbie Doll collection to my cousin, Collette, if the dolls are still in good condition." Again, there would be a problem with someone making an assessment. Who is to be the judge of what is a "good" condition for the collection?

If You Still Want to Make a Conditional Gift

So much for WillMaker rules. Despite the inherent problems, some people are determined to place conditions on beneficiaries or property. Occasionally, this can be sensibly accomplished with a custom-drafted clause. If you feel you must make a bequest with conditions, consult a lawyer who is experienced in drafting bequests that will adequately address these complex "what if" arrangements.

B. Naming a Beneficiary

The first step to making a specific bequest when using WillMaker is to name who is to receive it.

This is easy when the bequest you are making is to one individual: Type in the full name by which he or she is commonly known. This need not be the name that appears on a birth certificate; as long as the name you use clearly identifies the person in the context of your will, all is well.

Naming multiple beneficiaries to take one bequest is usually simple, too. Just list the names. However, in some circumstances, naming more than one beneficiary to take a specific bequest can be more complex. For instance, you may wish to:

- name beneficiaries to take property in unequal shares; or
- name one or more charitable institutions as beneficiaries.

1. Leaving Property in Equal Shares

If you want more than one beneficiary to share a specific bequest equally, simply list their names. WillMaker will automatically specify in your will that the beneficiaries should share the property equally.

▶ Running Out of Room

A very few people will find they are limited by the space allowed in the WillMaker program, which allows up to 212 characters to list the beneficiaries in every specific bequest screen. However, if you name many multiple beneficiaries, or beneficiaries with very long names, you may wish to be creative.

Example

When naming a group of twenty beneficiaries with the last name of Wyszymerinsky to inherit your cabin—which you will identify in a later screen—you might put "Chuck Wyszymerinsky, Isadora Wyszymerinsky, Ismerelda Wyszymerinsky, Salvator Wyszymerinsky and Natoli Wyszymerinsky" and so on. It is equally acceptable—and far less exhausting—to list these beneficiaries as "Chuck, Isadora, Ismerelda, Salvator and Natoli Wyszymerinsky."

2. Giving Property in Unequal Shares

As noted, if you name a group of beneficiaries without specifying the shares each should take, WillMaker automatically makes them equal. If you want one or more beneficiaries to receive a greater share of a particular item of property than the others, the best way to do this is to put the percentage in parentheses directly after each beneficiary's name. If you specify percentages, make sure that:

- each beneficiary is assigned a percentage; and

- the percentages add up to 100%.

Example

Fred Wagner wants to leave his ownership interest in an undeveloped real estate parcel to his three children—Mary, Sue and Peter. Because he has already paid for Mary's graduate school education, he wants to give Sue and Peter greater percentages of the property in case they want to go back to school, too. He lists his children and the share of his property to which they are entitled this way: Mary Wagner (20%), Sue Wagner (40%) and Peter Wagner (40%).

Alternatives for Multiple Beneficiaries

In most cases, you will not want to split up portions of a bequest by using several different screens. However, doing this can be extremely useful in multiple beneficiary situations if:

- you want to have a predeceased beneficiary's share go directly to a named alternate beneficiary instead of to his children or to the remaining beneficiaries; or

- you want to have one predeceased beneficiary's share pass to his children, another's share go to any remaining beneficiaries and another's share go to an alternate beneficiary.

Example

Pat wants to leave her cabin to her two children, Mike and Jim, and her sister Mary Lou. However, she wants each child to receive a 40% share and her sister a 20% share. In the event her children fail to survive her by 45 days, she wants their shares to go first to their children, if they have any, and otherwise to whichever one of them survives the other. However, if her sister predeceases her, Pat wants that 20% share to pass to her brother Roger rather than to either her sister's children or to Mike and Jim.

Using WillMaker, if Pat left her cabin to her children and her sister as multiple beneficiaries in one specific bequest, she could not accomplish what she wants to. If, however, Pat uses WillMaker to leave the cabin in three separate specific bequests, she can accomplish her goals with ease.

Pat would first name Mike as the beneficiary of a specific bequest. She would then use the property description screen to leave Mike a 40% interest in her cabin. Next, she would have this interest pass to Mike's children if Mike failed to survive her by 45 days. After finishing the bequest to Mike, Pat would do exactly the same for Jim. Finally, Pat would name Mary Lou as the beneficiary of a specific bequest, specify the property as 20% interest in the cabin, choose to have Mary Lou's share pass to a named alternate, and name Roger as the alternate. The following chart demonstrates this approach:

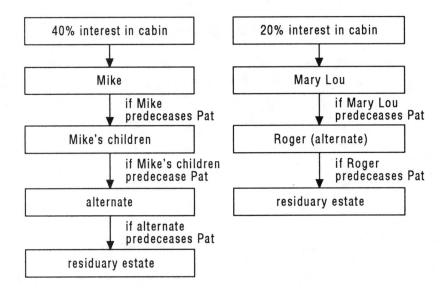

3. Charitable Institutions as Beneficiaries

You may want to name a charity or a public or private institution to take property in a specific bequest—for example, the American Red Cross, the Greenview Battered Women's Shelter, the University of Kansas. The institution you name need not be set up as a nonprofit, unless you wish your estate to qualify for a charitable estate tax deduction. (See Chapter 13, Section C.) It can be any organization you consider worthy of your bequest. The only limitation is that the institution must not be set up for some illicit or illegal purpose. For example, courts would likely find that the Downtown Center for Vice and Prostitution would not be eligible to inherit under a will.

When naming the charity you wish to take the bequest, be sure to enter its complete name, which may be different from the truncated version by which it is commonly known. Several different organizations may use similar names—and you want to be sure your bequest goes to the one you have in mind.

> **A Future Concern: Leaving Property to Minors or Young Adults**
> As you select your beneficiaries, keep in mind that property inherited by minors must be managed on their behalf until they become adults. Also, depending on the property and its value, you may want it managed until the beneficiary reaches an age well past 18. Later in the program, WillMaker offers a number of flexible ways to provide for this management. (See Chapter 7 for a detailed discussion.)

C. Describing Your Beneficiary

After you name each beneficiary, WillMaker asks you for a description. But it is not looking for a long-winded response. To answer, you need only type in the number next to the phrase that best describes your beneficiaries:

1. One individual

2. Two or more individuals

3. One or more charitable institutions

4. A mixture of individuals and institutions

WillMaker needs this information so that it can give you the opportunity to plan for the appropriate contingencies.

• If you have named only individuals to inherit the property, WillMaker will ask you to name an alternate beneficiary, who will get the property if your first choices do not survive you by the required period.

• If you have named a charitable institution as your first choice beneficiary, you will not be presented with the option of naming an alternate beneficiary. WillMaker makes the assumption that the charity will "survive" you—that is, it will still exist after your death.

- Finally, if you have named a mixture of individuals and institutions as beneficiaries of a specific bequest, you also need not name an alternate beneficiary. In such cases, WillMaker makes the assumption that even if the individuals you want to take the bequest do not survive, the institution will survive to take over all the property.

▶ Providing for Pets

You cannot legally name a pet as a beneficiary in your will; the law considers pets to be property. But if you own a pet, you may well be concerned that it receives a good home and good care after your death. Because of WillMaker's proscription against leaving bequests with conditions on them (see Section A2, above), you cannot leave, for example, "$100 to my sister Suzy, to be spent for my cat, Felix."

However, because a pet is legally considered to be property, you can leave it to another person in your will. It is also permissible to leave some money to the caretaker, explaining in a letter attached to your will that you want the money to be used for the pet's care. (See Chapter 12, Section A for a sample letter.) Of course, you should get the caretaker's agreement first—or he or she could end up as the unwilling recipient of an animal that needs care and a good home.

D. Describing Property in Bequest

Once you have described your beneficiaries, you are asked to describe the property you are leaving to them.

When describing a specific bequest, be as concise as you can. But use enough detail so that people will be able to identify and find the property. Most often, this will not be difficult: "my Baby Grand piano," "my collection of blue apothecary jars," "my llama throw rug" are all the description you will need for tangible items that are easy to locate.

> ### Do You Owe Money on Property You Are Leaving?
>
> It is common to pay for major assets such as a house, car, major appliances or a business over a period of time. For such assets, full payment is normally required to obtain full ownership. Also, assets you already own such as household furniture may be pledged as security for a loan or extension of credit.
>
> If you are leaving property in your will that carries an associated debt, you will naturally be concerned about whether the debt as well as the property should pass to the beneficiary, or whether the debt should be paid instead by your estate. WillMaker's handling of such concerns is discussed in detail in Chapter 9, but briefly:
>
> - WillMaker passes all debts owed on real estate, including mortgages, deeds of trust and tax liens, to the beneficiary of that real estate;
> - WillMaker passes all debts owed on personal property in connection with its purchase to the beneficiaries of the property; and
> - WillMaker provides that all debts owed on personal property for reasons other than its purchase—such as money you borrow from a finance company with your furniture pledged as collateral—shall be paid by your estate as you provide in your will.

If the property is very valuable or could be easily confused with other property, make sure you include identifying characteristics such as location, serial number, color or unique feature. If you have several high-tech machines you want to leave to different beneficiaries, for example, you can set out: "all my IBM computer equipment to Samuel Jones" and in another specific bequest, "all my Macintosh computer equipment to Samantha Jones."

Here is some help in how to identify different types of property with enough detail to prevent confusion:

- **Household furnishings** You normally need not get very specific here, unless some object is particularly valuable. It is enough to list the location of the property: "all household furnishings and possessions in the apartment at 55 Drury Lane."

- **Real estate** You can simply provide the street address, or for unimproved property, the name by which it is commonly known: "my condominium at 123 45th Avenue," "my summer home at 84 Memory Lane in Oakville," "the vacant lot next to the McHenry Place on Old Farm Road." You need not provide the legal description from the deed to it.

- **Bank, stock and money market accounts** List financial accounts by their account numbers. Also, include the name and location of the institution holding the property: "$20,000 from savings account #22222 at Independence Bank, Big Mountain, Idaho," "my money market account #23456 at Beryl Pynch & Company, Chicago, Illinois," "100 shares of General Foods common stock."

- **Personal Items** As with household goods, it is usually adequate to briefly describe personal items and group them, unless they have significant monetary or sentimental value. For example, items of extremely valuable jewelry should normally be listed and identified separately, while a drawer full of costume jewelry and baubles could be grouped.

What If There's Not Enough Space?

If you run out of room when describing a bequest you wish to give to the same beneficiaries, split it into two or more specific bequests.

Example

You want your collection of vintage coats to be shared by your two nieces, Doris and Natasha. Because each coat is special and valuable, you do not want to group them as "all my coats."

If the coats can be entered on the specific bequest screen by using 212 characters or less, you can list them all on one screen. However, if there are too many to fit on one WillMaker screen, you can deal with the problem as follows: Begin one bequest by naming Doris and Natasha as beneficiaries and describe several of the coats in the WillMaker screen titled Description of Bequest—"the aubergine silk smoking jacket, rose lace theater cape, paisley velvet blazer, red velour hunting jacket, handpainted kimono," and so on. After cycling through the options for naming alternate beneficiaries of this specific bequest, begin another bequest—again naming Doris and Natasha as beneficiaries and then listing the remainder of the coats.

▶ **WillMaker's Context Box:**
▶ **A Good Way to Check Your Wording**
▶   For short bequests, it is a good idea to doublecheck the wording of your bequest
▶   in the box at the bottom of the WillMaker screen to be sure the language you have
▶   chosen flows gracefully in the context of your completed will. If your bequest is
▶   too long to appear in the context box in its complete form, check the wording
▶   when you display your will on the screen or when you print it out.

E.   What If a Beneficiary Dies Before You Do?

After you describe the property that you are leaving in a bequest, WillMaker asks you to consider the possibility that your first choice as beneficiary will not survive you by 45 days, except for your spouse, for whom there is no survivorship period. In this screen, you indicate your broad plan as to who gets your property if your first choice beneficiary fails to survive you by 45 days. If this involves naming an alternate beneficiary, you will have the opportunity to do that on the next screen.

1. One Beneficiary

If the beneficiary is one individual, and he or she does not survive you by 45 days—and so is disqualified by the will from taking the bequest—you can peg that individual's share to go to:

- his or her children in equal shares; or
- one or more alternate beneficiaries to be named on the next screen.

2. Two or More Beneficiaries

If you have named two or more beneficiaries to share a specific bequest, and one of them fails to survive you by the 45-day period, you can have that individual's share of the property go to:

- his or her children; or
- the surviving first choice beneficiaries.

If you have named a charitable institution as beneficiary, you will not be presented with alternate beneficiary screens. The assumption is that the charitable institution will survive you.

(See Section L of this chapter for an explanation of how to arrange for a contingency plan that will work according to your wishes.)

F. Alternate Beneficiaries

Here, you are allowed to name one or more alternate beneficiaries to take the bequest if your first choice—and back-up choices, if you named them—do not survive for the required period.

Example

Joan leaves her horse to her brother Pierre. In case Pierre does not survive her by 45 days to take this bequest, Joan names her sister Carmen to get the horse as the alternate beneficiary.

Example

Gideon leaves his house to his three nephews in equal shares. In case one or more of the nephews fails to survive him by 45 days, Gideon specifies that the house go to the surviving nephews in equal shares. He names his brother Morris as alternate beneficiary. Morris will get the house only if none of the nephews survive Gideon by 45 days.

If you want two or more people to share one piece of property but want to name different alternate beneficiaries for any of them, use separate screens to break apart the bequest.

Example

Marcia wants to leave her home to her two children, Emily and Robb. If Emily does not survive to take the bequest, Marcia wants Emily's share to go to Emily's two children. If Robb, who is unmarried and has no children, does not survive, Marcia wants his share to go to the Red Cross. The best way for her to put this plan in place using WillMaker would be to make two separate specific bequests to each of her children. The property in each bequest would be described as: "1/2 my home at 27998 SE Moss Street." Then she could name different alternate beneficiaries for each bequest.

G. List Of Beneficiaries

When you complete a specific bequest—that is, you have named the beneficiary, identified the property and named an alternate beneficiary—WillMaker will display the first choice beneficiary's name on the screen. You can then add, review or change and delete any one of the bequests by following the instructions at the bottom of the screen.

Assuming you wish to make a second specific bequest, choose the "add" option. Then complete the cycle again until you have made all your specific bequests—up to a maximum of 28 in all.

H. Leaving Your Residuary Estate

Your "residuary estate" is all the property you own at your death but for which you have not named a beneficiary in your will and have not arranged to pass to anyone outside the will by means of a probate avoidance technique, such as joint tenancy or a living trust. (See Chapter 13 for an overview of these techniques.) Your residuary estate can include property you overlook when making your will, property that comes into your hands after you make your will and property that does not go to the person you named to get it in a specific bequest, for example, because that person dies before you do and you have not named an alternate beneficiary to receive the property.

If you make few specific bequests, your residuary estate can contain a great deal of property—the value of which can increase substantially from the time you write your will until the time you die. But it can also decrease in value because you spend or give away the property that would have been passed in it.

▶ **Debts and Taxes: Your Residuary Estate Often Must Pay**
After your death, property in the residuary is often what is used to satisfy unsecured debts, unpaid income taxes and estate taxes you owe at your death unless you specify otherwise in your will. Secured debts such as mortgages and car payments pass with the specific item of property. (See Chapter 9 for a thorough discussion of debts and taxes and why it is often wise to use your will to identify specific funds to pay them.)

You can name one or more individuals, one or more institutions or a combination of individuals and institutions to take your residuary estate. If more than one residuary beneficiary is named, WillMaker will make the assumption that you intend for them to share the residuary property equally. If you want them to take unequal shares, you must specify that after their names.

Example

Maurice Fuhrmann leaves his residuary estate to his five children—Clara, Heinrich, Franz, Lise and Wiebke. He wants Lise and Wiebke each to receive 35% of the property and the other three children to receive 10% each. He should list the children this way on the screen asking him to name his residuary beneficiary: Clara Fuhrmann (10%), Heinrich Fuhrmann (10%), Franz Fuhrmann (10%), Lise Fuhrmann (35%) and Wiebke Fuhrmann (35%).

If you use this approach, make sure every beneficiary has a percentage and that the percentages add up to 100%.

Example

Ted and Mary Edwards, a married couple with two children, make no specific bequests in their wills. Instead, they each name the other as residuary beneficiary, which means the survivor takes all of the property when the first spouse dies. Each names the two children as alternate residuary beneficiaries.

I. Describe Your Residuary Beneficiaries

WillMaker next asks you to describe the beneficiaries you have named to take your residuary estate.

If you indicate that you have chosen an individual or two or more individuals to take your residuary estate, WillMaker will ask you to think ahead and indicate your broad plan as to who gets your property if your first choice does not survive you by 45 days. If this involves naming an alternate residuary beneficiary, you will have the opportunity to do that on the next screen.

Remember that, using WillMaker, all beneficiaries except for your spouse must survive you by 45 days to take property under your will. If your first choice as a residuary beneficiary is one individual and he or she fails to survive you by 45 days, WillMaker allows you to choose for the property to go to either:

- that residuary beneficiary's children, in equal shares; or

- one or more alternate residuary beneficiaries you can name on the next screen.

Example

Alfredo leaves his residuary estate to his daughter Vanessa. He then specifies that if Vanessa does not survive him, her share should go to her two children—Alfredo's grandchildren. If Vanessa dies before Alfredo, and he does not write a new will, Vanessa's children would each inherit one-half of Alfredo's residuary estate.

Example

Jack writes a WillMaker will, making a few specific bequests to relatives and leaving his residuary estate to his friend Joe. He names his other friend Josette as alternate residuary beneficiary. Josette will inherit property under Jack's will only if Joe does not survive 45 days longer than Jack.

If you have chosen a charitable institution to take all or part of your residuary estate, you need not worry about naming any alternate to take your residuary estate. WillMaker simply assumes the institution will survive, that is, be in operation longer than 45 days after you die, so will take your residuary estate.

J. Alternate Residuary Beneficiaries

It is a good idea to name one or more people or institutions as alternate residuary beneficiaries to provide a kind of insurance against the bleak scenario that all other beneficiaries die before you. Your alternate residuary beneficiaries will take the property left in your residuary estate if no other named beneficiaries survive to take it.

K. Simultaneous Death of Spouses

Many people—especially married couples with children—are concerned about what will happen to their property and their children in the unlikely event that they both die at the same time.

Occasionally, spouses do die at the same time in an accident or other catastrophe, and it is impossible to determine who died first. When this happens, WillMaker wills automatically apply the assumption that the maker of the will has survived his or her spouse. Although this may seen logically inconsistent—after all, they cannot both have outlived the other—it is perfectly legal, because each will is considered independently. And the result is a fair one. The husband's estate will pass to his heirs or the alternate beneficiaries named in his will and the wife's property will pass to hers. Otherwise, there would be the risk that one spouse's property would pass through the other's estate. That would result in the same property being probated twice.

Typically, married couples with children will leave all or most of their property to their spouse, naming the children as alternate beneficiaries.

Example

Don and Melanie, a married couple, have two young children. Each uses WillMaker to make their wills—leaving all their property to one another by naming each other to take their residuary estates. They name no alternate beneficiaries. They then name a manager to handle the property for their children should they inherit before they reach an age at which they are legally capable of getting it outright. A short time later, Don and Melanie die in the same plane crash. Under the simultaneous death clause of their WillMaker wills, neither Melanie's nor Don's property will pass to the other, but instead will go directly to their children.

L. Who Gets the Property If Your First Choices Do Not Survive?

Making a will is easy if your primary concern is to designate who should get your property as a first choice. But things can get murky in a hurry if you want to provide for the fateful possibility that your first choice or choices will fail to survive you by the required period—45 days for all beneficiaries other than a spouse.

Not everyone is concerned about this issue. Younger people in reasonably good health are usually confident that they can address a beneficiary's premature death by updating their will. However, married people are commonly concerned about what will happen if they die in close proximity. And older people in poor health are concerned that they will not have an opportunity to update their wills if their first choice beneficiaries die before they do.

This section provides some examples of how you can use WillMaker to plan for the contingency of a beneficiary's death.

1. Specific Bequests to an Individual Beneficiary

After you have made a specific bequest of property to an individual beneficiary, WillMaker offers a choice as to what happens in the event that beneficiary fails to survive you by 45 days. You can choose to have the property pass:

1. to the first choice beneficiary's children in equal shares, or

2. directly to one or more alternate beneficiaries you name on a later screen.

Option #1: Property First to Children and Then to Alternate

Example

Janie makes a will leaving most of her estate to her husband and certain family heirlooms to their child Ellen. Janie designates Ellen's children to inherit the heirlooms if Ellen doesn't survive her, and names her husband as the alternate beneficiary. Ellen fails to survive Janie by 45 days, but leaves three children of her own.

Assuming Janie does not change her will, the grandchildren inherit the heirlooms in equal shares. However, if none of the grandchildren survive Janie by 45 days, her husband, as alternate beneficiary, receives the heirlooms. If no alternate had been named or the alternate (Janie's husband) failed to survive Janie, the heirlooms would have gone into Janie's residuary estate. The following chart shows how this works:

To beneficiary's children

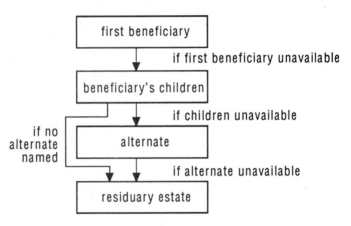

Option #2: Property Directly to Alternate

As mentioned, if you do not choose to have your beneficiary's children inherit the property in the event the beneficiary predeceases you, but instead direct it to go to the alternate, you merely shorten the chain of potential beneficiaries. The basic scheme is the same, but the property will go directly to the alternate beneficiary you choose if the first beneficiary is unavailable. If the alternate also does not survive you, the property will become part of your residuary estate.

Example

Sal makes out a will leaving one specific bequest of her antique piano to her brother Tim. She then names her daughter Justine as residuary beneficiary, which means Justine receives everything but the piano. Sal does not want Tim's children to receive the piano in the event Tim fails to survive her, so she does not choose WillMaker option #1, but instead makes choice #2 and names her sister Val as alternate beneficiary.

If Tim fails to survive Sal by 45 days, the piano will go to Val. Tim's children will not get it. If Val also fails to survive Sal, the piano will go to Justine, Sal's residuary beneficiary.

To alternate beneficiary

```
                    ┌─────────────────────────┐
                    │   first beneficiary     │
                    └─────────────────────────┘
                              │      if first beneficiary unavailable
    if no                     ▼
  alternate         ┌─────────────────────────┐
    named           │       alternate         │
                    └─────────────────────────┘
                              │      if alternate unavailable
                    ▼         ▼
                    ┌─────────────────────────┐
                    │    residuary estate     │
                    └─────────────────────────┘
```

2. Specific Bequests to Multiple Beneficiaries

When the original bequest is made to two or more beneficiaries, choosing alternate beneficiaries becomes slightly more complicated. If one of a group of beneficiaries dies, WillMaker gives you two options.

Option #1: Property First to Children, Then to Alternates

Under the first option, the property goes first to the surviving children, if any exist, of the deceased beneficiary, in equal shares. If there are no surviving children, the property goes to any surviving beneficiaries in equal shares. If there are no other surviving beneficiaries, the property goes next to an alternate if one has been named. If none has been named, the property passes into the residuary estate.

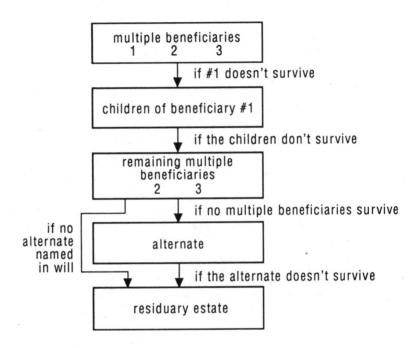

Example

Pat leaves her vacation cabin in the mountains to her children Mike and Jim and her sister Mary Lou. Should neither Jim nor Mary Lou survive Pat by 45 days, Pat chooses to specify that the children of named beneficiaries receive their shares. This means that if Jim and Mary Lou fail to survive Pat, Jim's two children would take his share, and Mary Lou's son takes Mary Lou's share.

If neither the named beneficiaries nor any of their children had survived Pat, the person Pat named as the alternate beneficiary would take the bequest. If no alternate was named, the cabin would have become part of Pat's residuary estate.

Example

Myrna has three children, Abby, Ben and Charlotte. She leaves the contents of her savings account to them in equal shares. Myrna uses WillMaker to specify that should any of them not survive her by 45 days, that child's share will go to his or her surviving children (Myrna's grandchildren) and that, if there are no surviving children, to the remaining named beneficiaries—for example, if Ben dies before Myrna, to Abby and Charlotte. At Myrna's death, the savings account contains $30,000. First, assume that Ben predeceased Myrna and left no children. His share would be split between Abby and Charlotte, who will each get $15,000. Abby and Charlotte have two children each, who will receive nothing; the only grandchildren entitled to Ben's share are his children, and none survived him.

Now assume that both Abby and Ben predeceased Myrna. In that case, Abby's one-third share would be split equally by her children. Charlotte, the only surviving child, would receive $20,000—her share and Ben's share, since she is the sole surviving named beneficiary.

Next assume that Abby, Ben, Charlotte and one of Charlotte's children predeceased Myrna. In this case, because all three primary beneficiaries have predeceased Myrna, only the surviving grandchildren inherit. Abby's kids would split her original $10,000 share, Charlotte's kids would take her entire share, and Ben's share would pass into Myrna's residuary estate unless she had named an alternate.

Finally, if all of the children and grandchildren had predeceased Myrna, the named alternate would take the $30,000. If no alternate had been named, the money would go into the residuary estate.

Note   Remember that when you choose the multiple beneficiaries option, you can specify only children, not grandchildren, of a named beneficiary to take their parent's share of a bequest. If your will becomes so out-of-date that not only a beneficiary, but all the beneficiary's children predecease you, any grandchildren of the beneficiary are out of luck. They will not inherit anything; the beneficiary's share will go to surviving named beneficiaries, the alternate, or the residuary estate.

Option #2: Property Direct to Surviving Beneficiaries

The other way of dealing with multiple beneficiaries using WillMaker simply involves the person making a will choosing to bypass the children of the named beneficiaries. Under this approach, a deceased beneficiary's share is divided among the other multiple beneficiaries. If none of the original multiple beneficiaries survives, the bequest passes to the alternate beneficiary named in the will. In the unlikely event that none of the named beneficiaries or the alternate survives you, the property becomes part of the residuary estate.

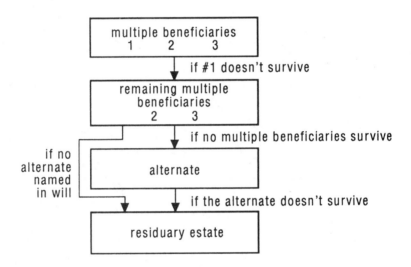

Example

Brandy uses WillMaker to provide in her will that her house will be divided equally between her brother Zeke and her daughter Maria. Her will also specifies that if one of the beneficiaries dies within 45 days after Brandy's death, his or her share will go to the other beneficiary, not to his or her children. Brandy chooses her friend Sabrina as the alternate beneficiary. Maria dies before Brandy, leaving two children.

Zeke, the surviving beneficiary, gets Maria's share of the property. Maria's children take nothing. If Zeke and Maria had both died before Brandy—and Brandy had not made a new will—Sabrina would inherit the property. If Sabrina had not survived Brandy, the property would go to the residuary estate.

6 Structured Solutions for Simple Wills

Solution 1
No children or grandchildren
All property to spouse

Solution 2
Adult children of the marriage
No deceased children
All property to spouse
Children as alternates in equal shares
Property to beneficiaries of your choice
  if spouse and children do not survive

Solution 3
Minor children
No deceased children
All property to spouse
Minor children as alternates
  in equal shares

Solution 1
No children or deceased children
All property to one adult individual
  or charitable institution

Solution 2
Adult children
All property to one adult individual
  as beneficiary
Adult children as alternates

Solution 3
Adult children
All property to children in
  equal shares
Grandchildren as alternate
  beneficiaries

Solution 4
Minor children
No deceased children
All property to children in equal shares
One person or charitable institution
  as alternate

WillMaker offers considerable flexibility to meet the needs of people with detailed plans for leaving their property. For example, you can make 28 separate specific bequests of property. And if you wish, you can name multiple beneficiaries for each and provide that a beneficiary's children take his or her share if the beneficiary does not survive you by 45 days. You can also name an alternate beneficiary to provide a second level of back-up. Even though WillMaker offers a wide range of choices, if you know what property you have and who you want to leave it to, it is possible to produce a completed will in less than an hour.

A. Who Should Use this Chapter

Some people find the flexibility offered by WillMaker a little vexing. To them, there are just too many choices to think through. Fortunately, there is often an alternative if your main goal is to get a very simple will written quickly. It consists of this chapter's screen-by-screen guidance through the program in the situations set out in the table of contents at the beginning of the chapter.

The instructions here are appropriate only when your willmaking wishes are limited to leaving all your property to one or a small group of beneficiaries, naming a personal representative (executor) to handle your estate and possibly naming a personal guardian for minor children.

Do not use this chapter if you:

- plan to leave valuable property to minor children;

- have any deceased children;

- want to spread your property among a number of beneficiaries; or

- want to carefully plan for the possibility that one or more of your beneficiaries won't survive you.

B. How to Use this Chapter

The instructions set out in this chapter make your willmaking task easier by making a number of decisions for you in the seven simple situations. They let you bypass many screens—particularly those containing complicated choices.

 Follow Structured Solutions Exactly

Because you are trading your own decisions with our instructions, it is important to follow them to the letter. If you find you want more flexibility than you are being given, use the program from the beginning and proceed through it screen-by-screen, instead. WillMaker is not difficult to use and there is no sense in locking in to any Structured Solution unless it fits your needs exactly.

Each instruction line tells you what to do on the program screen that it addresses. When you are finished with one instruction, proceed to the next WillMaker screen—by clicking on either Next Screen or OK—and follow the instructions for that screen. You may obtain additional information about each screen by selecting Help from the Options menu.

By using the Structured Solutions offered in this chapter, you will skip through initial screens in the program that describe background information, WillMaker help functions and program operations.

If, when following the instructions in this chapter, you discover that your needs are more complex than you originally thought, or you get confused about where you are in the willmaking process, go to the File menu and choose Erase and Start Over. This will erase what you have done so far and return you to the beginning of the program—where you can take full advantage of WillMaker's options and informed guidance.

C. If You Are Married

Solution 1

Married

No children or grandchildren

All property to spouse

Example

Peter and Lois Smyth are married. They are both 32. They have no children but hope to have them soon. They own considerable equity in their house, some valuable antique furniture and a joint savings account. Each makes a will leaving all their property to the other. Peter's will lists his father and mother as alternate beneficiaries in case Lois fails to survive him. Lois lists her best friend Barbara as alternate beneficiary in case Peter dies before she does. Peter and Lois understand that if they do have children, they should make new wills that include them.

1. Start WillMaker. If you don't know how to do this, see Section A at the beginning of this Users' Guide.

2. The first screen you will see is "Welcome to WillMaker."

3. Go to the Options menu and select Skip Info Screens. This will signal WillMaker to skip all information screens and show only screens that require you to enter information or answer questions. Then proceed with the program by clicking on Next Screen.

4. **Name**   Enter your name as you do on formal documents, first name first. When you are satisfied with your answer, click OK to move on to the next screen in the program.

5. **Social Security Number**   Enter your Social Security number if you wish. It is optional but it may help your personal representative identify your accounts and other property. Click OK.

6. **State**   Click on your state. Then click OK.

7. **County**   Enter your county as you wish it to appear in your will—such as "Caledonia County" or "County of Orange." Remember to include the

word county—or its equivalent if you live in a state that uses a different term. Click OK.

8. **Are You Married?** Click on Yes. Then click OK.

9. **Spouse's Name** Enter the name your spouse is using in his or her will or on other formal documents. Click OK.

10. **Do You Have Children?** Click on No, then OK.

11. **Children of Deceased Children?** Click on No, then OK.

12. **Specific Bequests** Click on No; you do not wish to make any specific bequests. Then click on OK.

13. **Leaving Your Residuary Estate** Enter your spouse's name, using the same form you did when you entered it earlier. When you have entered it correctly, click on OK.

14, **Describe Beneficiary** Click on the button next to the top choice to indicate an individual. Click OK.

15. **If Your Residuary Beneficiary Dies Before You** Click on the bottom button to indicate the property should go to the alternate to be named on the next screen if your first choice fails to survive you. Click OK.

16. **Alternate Residuary Beneficiary** Enter the name of one or more beneficiaries of your choice as alternates to take your property in equal shares if your spouse fails to survive you. When you are satisfied that you have entered your answers properly, click on OK.

17. **Have You Named a Minor to Receive Property under Your Will?** Click on No so that you will be routed past the screens that let you provide property management for minor beneficiaries.

Think Twice about Management

If you named a minor as an alternate residuary beneficiary, any property he or she inherits while still a minor will have to be managed by an adult. If you do not arrange for such management in your will, the court will appoint and supervise a property guardian. Generally, the court-appointed guardian approach is not recommended.

However, using WillMaker to set up property management of minors requires some thought and a number of choices. Because your spouse is your first choice beneficiary for all your property, setting up management for the possibility that a minor will inherit is not crucial—especially for younger willmakers who are likely to live for years. However if you want to provide it, answer Yes to this question. Then go to the Options menu, de-select Skip Info Screens, and carefully proceed through the rest of the program.

18. **Property Management for Young Adults?** Click on No, then OK.

19. **Name a Personal Representative** Enter the name of one trusted adult to manage your estate—to distribute your property and pay your debts and taxes. After you are satisfied that the name is entered correctly, click OK.

20. **Alternate Personal Representative** Enter the name of your choice for alternate personal representative. Then click OK.

21. **Do You Want to Cancel Any Debts?** Click on No, then OK.

22. **Select How to Pay Debts and Expenses** Click on No, then OK.

23. **Select How to Pay Taxes** Click on No, then OK.

24. At this point, you will have entered all the information required for your will. A dialog box will appear, informing you that you can now print your completed will. When you are finished reading the box, click OK. You will next see the screen that enables you to review or modify any portion of your completed will. If you wish to doublecheck your will by reading it on the screen, go to the File menu and select Preview Will.

25. To print your will, open the File menu and select Print All Documents. You will next see directions on your screen from your individual software, informing you about printing options.

26. Carefully follow the instructions that print out with your will. If a "self-proving affidavit" also prints out, ignore it for now. It helps to get your will admitted to the probate court, but it is not necessary to make a valid will, and does you no good if you are relatively young and will make a number of subsequent wills before you die. Later, if you wish, you can round up at least two of your witnesses and sign the affidavit in front of a Notary Public.

Solution 2

Married
Adult children of the marriage
No deceased children
All property to spouse
Children as alternates in equal shares
Property to beneficiaries of your choice if spouse
    and children do not survive

Example

Ray and Monica are married. Both are 64 years old. They have three children—all alive and over 30. Ray and Monica rent an apartment which they have furnished with a valuable collection of modern art. They also own an active investment portfolio, a bank account in joint tenancy, two cars and assorted personal property. Ray and Monica each make a separate will, leaving their own share of the property to the other. Ray's will specifies that the children should take the property in equal shares if Monica fails to survive him, and Monica's will has the same provision if Ray fails to survive her. Ray names his brother Tom to take his share of the property if neither Monica nor the children survive him, and Monica names her sister Tina to take her property under the same circumstances.

1. Start WillMaker. If you don't know how to do this, see Section A at the beginning of this Users' Guide.

2. The first screen you will see is "Welcome to WillMaker."

3. Go to the Options menu and select Skip Info Screens. This will signal WillMaker to skip all information screens and show only screens that require you to enter information or answer questions. Then proceed with the program by clicking on Next Screen.

4. **Name** Enter your name as you do on formal documents, first name first. When you are satisfied with your answer, click OK to move on to the next screen in the program.

5. **Social Security Number** Enter your Social Security number if you wish. It is optional but it may help your personal representative identify your accounts and other property. Click OK.

6. **State** Click on your state. Then click OK.

7. **County**   Enter your county as you wish it to appear in your will—such as "Caledonia County" or "County of Orange." Remember to include the word county—or its equivalent if you live in a state that uses a different term. Click OK.

8. **Are You Married**?   Click on Yes. Then click OK.

9. **Spouse's Name**   Enter the name your spouse is using in his or her will or on other formal documents. Click OK.

10. **Children**   Click on Yes, then OK.

11. **Children's Names**   Enter the full names of your children, first name first. If there is insufficient room, use middle initials or first name abbreviations. When you are finished making all entries, click on OK.

12. **Minor Children?** Click onn No, then OK.

13. **Children of Deceased Children?** Click on No, then OK.

14. **Specific Bequests**   Click on No; you do not wish to make specific bequests. Then click OK.

15. **Leaving Your Residuary Estate**   Enter your spouse's name, using the same form you did when you entered it earlier. After you have entered the name correctly, click on OK.

16. **Describe Beneficiary**   Click on the button next to the top choice to indicate an individual. Click OK.

17. **If Your Residuary Beneficiary Dies Before You**   Click on the top button to indicate the property should go to the children of your marriage as alternate beneficiaries in case your spouse does not survive you. Then click OK.

18. **Alternate Residuary Beneficiary**   Enter the name of one or more alternate beneficiaries to take your property if your spouse and children fail to survive you. These may be your grandchildren, other relatives or friends, or a charitable institution. When you are satisfied that you have entered your answers properly, click OK.

19. **Have You Named a Minor to Receive Property under Your Will?** Click on No so that you will be routed past the screens that let you provide property management for minors.

Think Twice about Management

If you named a minor as an alternate residuary beneficiary, any property he or she inherits while still a minor will have to be managed by an adult. If you do not arrange for such management in your will, the court will appoint and supervise a property guardian. Generally, the court-appointed guardian approach is not recommended.

However, using WillMaker to set up property management of minors requires some thought and a number of choices. Because your spouse is your first choice beneficiary for all your property, setting up management for the possibility that a minor will inherit is not crucial—especially for younger willmakers who are likely to live for years. However if you want to provide it, answer Yes to this question. Then go to the Options menu, de-select Skip Info Screens, and carefully proceed through the rest of the program.

20. **Property Management for Young Adults?** Click on No, then OK.

    If you would not want your adult children to receive the property without it being managed in a trust, answer Yes to this question. Then go to the Options menu, de-select Skip Info Screens, and proceed through the rest of the program.

21. **Name a Personal Representative** Enter the name of one trusted adult to manage your estate—to distribute your property and pay your debts and taxes. After you are satisfied that the name is entered correctly, click OK.

22. **Alternate Personal Representative** Enter the name of your choice for alternate personal representative. Then click OK.

23. **Do You Want to Cancel Any Debts?** Click on No, then OK.

24. **Select How to Pay Debts and Expenses** Click on No, then OK.

25. **Select How to Pay Taxes** Click on No, then OK.

26. At this point, you will have entered all the information required for your will. A dialog box will appear, informing you that you can now print your completed will. When you are finished reading the box, click OK. You will next see the screen that enables you to review or modify any portion of your completed will. If you wish to doublecheck your will by reading it on the screen, go to the File menu and select Preview Will.

27. To print your will, open the File menu and select Print All Documents. You will next see directions on your screen from your individual software, informing you about printing options.

28. Carefully follow the instructions that print out with your will. If a "self-proving affidavit" also prints out, ignore it for now. It helps to get your will admitted to the probate court, but it is not necessary to make a valid will, and does you no good if you are relatively young and will make a number of subsequent wills before you die. Later, if you wish, you can round up at least two of your witnesses and sign the affidavit in front of a Notary Public.

Solution 3

Married
Minor children
No deceased children
All property to spouse
Minor children as alternates in equal shares

Example

Mick and Lorraine are married. Both are 35. They have three children—14, 10 and 6. Mick and Lorraine own a small home, a valuable Steinway grand piano—inherited by Mick from his pianist grandfather—a bank account in joint tenancy, cars and assorted personal property. Mick and Lorraine each make a will leaving their shares of the property to the other. Mick's will specifies that the children should take the property in equal shares if Lorraine fails to survive him, and Lorraine's will does likewise if Mick fails to survive her. Mick names his brother Leroy to take his share of the property if neither Lorraine nor the children survive him, and Lorraine names her sister Sally to take her property under the same circumstances.

1. Start WillMaker. If you don't know how to do this, see Section A at the beginning of this Users' Guide.

2. The first screen you will see is "Welcome to WillMaker."

3. Go to the Options menu and select Skip Info Screens. This will signal WillMaker to skip all information screens and show only screens that

require you to enter information or answer questions. Then proceed with the program by clicking on Next Screen.

4. **Name**   Enter your name as you do on formal documents, first name first. When you are satisfied with your answer, click OK to move on to the next screen in the program.

5. **Social Security Number**   Enter your Social Security number if you wish. It is optional but it may help your personal representative identify your accounts and other property. Click OK.

6. **State**   Click on your state. Then click OK.

7. **County**   Enter your county as you wish it to appear in your will—such as "Caledonia County" or "County of Orange." Remember to include the word county—or its equivalent if you live in a state that uses a different term. Click OK.

8. **Are You Married**?   Click on Yes. Then click OK.

9. **Spouse's Name**   Enter the name your spouse is using in his or her will or on other formal documents. Click OK.

10. **Children**   Click on Yes, then OK.

11. **Children's Names**   Enter the full names of your children, first name first. If there is insufficient room, use middle initials or first name abbreviations. When you are finished making all entries, click on OK.

12. **Minor Children?** Click on Yes, then OK.

13. **Children of Deceased Children?** Click on No, then OK.

14. **Specific Bequests**   Answer N; you do not wish to make specific bequests. Then click OK.

15. **Leaving Your Residuary Estate**   Enter your spouse's name, using the same form you did when you entered it earlier. After you have entered it correctly, click OK.

16. **Describe Beneficiary**   Click on the button next to the top choice to indicate an individual. Click OK.

17. **If Your Residuary Beneficiary Dies Before You**   Click on the top button to indicate the property should go to the children of your marriage as alternate beneficiaries in case your spouse does not survive you. Then click OK.

18. **Alternate Residuary Beneficiary**   Enter the name of one or more alternate beneficiaries to take your property if your spouse and children fail to survive you. These may be your grandchildren, other relatives or friends, or a charitable institution. When you are satisfied that you have entered your answers properly, click OK.

19. **Personal Guardian**   Enter the name of a close relative or friend to be personal guardian of your minor children in case you and your spouse die close together in time. After you have entered the name correctly, click OK.

20. **Alternate Personal Guardian**   Enter the name of an alternate personal guardian—perhaps the spouse of the person you named as your first choice. If you don't want to name an alternate, click OK.

21. **Have You Named a Minor to Receive Property under Your Will?** Click on No so that you will be routed past the screens that let you provide property management for minors. But heed the caution set out below.

Think Twice about Management

If you named a minor as an alternate residuary beneficiary, any property he or she inherits while still a minor will have to be managed by an adult. If you do not arrange for such management in your will, the court will appoint and supervise a property guardian. Generally, the court-appointed guardian approach is not recommended.

However, using WillMaker to set up property management of minors requires some thought and a number of choices. Because your spouse is your first choice beneficiary for all your property, setting up management for the possibility that a minor will inherit is not crucial—especially for younger willmakers who are likely to live for years. However if you want to provide it, answer Yes to this question. Then click on OK, and carefully proceed through the rest of the program.

22. **Property Management for Young Adults?**   Click on No, then OK. If you would not want your adult children to receive the property without it being managed in a trust, answer Y to this question. Then go to the Options menu, de-select Skip Info Screens, and carefully proceed through the rest of the program.

23. **Name a Personal Representative** Enter the name of one trusted adult to manage your estate—to distribute your property and pay your debts and taxes. After you are satisfied that the name is entered correctly, click OK.

24. **Alternate Personal Representative** Enter the name of your choice for alternate personal representative. Then click OK.

25. **Do You Want to Cancel Any Debts?** Click on No, then OK.

26. **Select How to Pay Debts and Expenses** Click on No, then OK.

27. **Select How to Pay Taxes** Click on No, then OK.

28. At this point, you will have entered all the information required for your will. A dialog box will appear, informing you that you can now print your completed will. When you are finished reading the box, click OK. You will next see the screen that enables you to review or modify any portion of your completed will. If you wish to doublecheck your will by reading it on the screen, go to the File menu and select Preview Will.

29. To print your will, open the File menu and select Print All Documents. You will next see directions on your screen from your individual software, informing you about printing options.

30. Carefully follow the instructions that print out with your will. If a "self-proving affidavit" also prints out, ignore it for now. It helps to get your will admitted to the probate court, but it is not necessary to make a valid will, and does you no good if you are relatively young and will make a number of subsequent wills before you die. Later, if you wish, you can round up at least two of your witnesses and sign the affidavit in front of a Notary Public.

B. If You Are Unmarried

Solution 1

Unmarried

No children or deceased children

All property to one adult individual or charitable institution

Example

Peter and Clarence are life companions. They are both 32. Neither has any children. They jointly own a house, some valuable sound recording equipment, a bank account in joint tenancy, expensive stereo equipment, two cars and assorted personal property. Each makes a will leaving all their property to the other. Peter's will lists his father and mother as alternate beneficiaries in case Clarence fails to survive him. Clarence's will lists a close friend as alternate in case Peter dies before he does.

Example

Grover is 58 and a widower. He has no children. He owns a house, a stock portfolio, car and assorted personal property. He makes a will leaving all his property to the National Cancer Institute.

Example

Same as Example 2 except Grover leaves all his property to his only brother, Sam. He names the National Cancer Institute as alternate beneficiary in case Sam fails to survive him.

1. Start WillMaker. If you don't know how to do this, see Section A at the beginning of this Users' Guide.

2. The first screen you will see is "Welcome to WillMaker."

3. Go to the Options menu and select Skip Info Screens. This will signal WillMaker to skip all information screens and show only screens that require you to enter information or answer questions. Then proceed with the program by clicking on Next Screen.

4. **Name** Enter your name as you do on formal documents, first name first. When you are satisfied with your answer, click OK to move on to the next screen in the program.

5. **Social Security Number** Enter your Social Security number if you wish. It is optional but it may help your personal representative identify your accounts and other property. Click OK.

6. **State** Click on your state. Then click OK.

7. **County** Enter your county as you wish it to appear in your will—such as "Caledonia County" or "County of Orange." Remember to include the word county—or its equivalent if you live in a state that uses a different term. Click OK.

10. **Are You Married?** Click No, then OK.

11. **Do You Have Children?** Click No, then OK.

12. **Children of Deceased Children?** Click No, then OK.

13. **Specific Bequests** Click No; you do not wish to make specific bequests. Then click OK.

14. **Leaving Your Residuary Estate** Enter the name of one adult individual or a charitable institution to receive all your property. For an individual, use the name by which he or she is commonly known. When you are satisfied that the name has been entered correctly, click OK.

15. **Describe Beneficiary** Click on the button next to the choice that accurately describes your beneficiary. Then click OK.

16. **If Your Residuary Beneficiary Dies Before You** (*This screen will only appear if the beneficiary you selected in instruction 15 is an individual.*)

    Click on the bottom button to indicate the property should go to the alternate to be named on the next screen if your first choice does not survive you.

17. **Alternate Residuary Beneficiary** (*This screen will only appear if the beneficiary you selected in instruction 15 is an individual.*)

    Enter the name of one or more beneficiaries as alternates to take your property in equal shares if your first choice fails to survive you. When you are satisfied that the names you have entered are correct, click OK.

18. **Have you Named a Minor to Receive Property under Your Will?** Click on No so that you will be routed past the screens that let you provide property management for minors. But heed the caution set out below.

Think Twice about Management

If you named a minor as an alternate residuary beneficiary, any property he or she inherits while still a minor will have to be managed by an adult. If you do not arrange for such management in your will, the court will appoint and supervise a property guardian. Generally, the court-appointed guardian approach is not recommended.

However, using WillMaker to set up property management of minors requires some thought and a number of choices. Because an adult individual or a charitable institution is your first choice beneficiary for all your property, setting up management for the possibility that a minor will inherit is not crucial—especially for younger willmakers who are likely to live for years. However if you want to provide it, answer Yes to this question. Then go to the Options menu, de-select Skip Info Screens, and carefully proceed through the rest of the program.

19. **Property Management for Young Adults?** Click No, then OK.

20. **Name a Personal Representative**   Enter the name of one trusted adult to manage your estate—to distribute your property and pay your debts and taxes. After you are satisfied that the name is entered correctly, click OK.

21. **Alternate Personal Representative**   Enter the name of your choice for alternate personal representative. Then click OK.

22. **Do You Want to Cancel Any Debts?** Click on No, then OK.

23. **Select How to Pay Debts and Expenses**   Click on No, then OK.

24. **Select How to Pay Taxes**   Click on No, then OK.

25. At this point, you will have entered all the information required for your will. A dialog box will appear, informing you that you can now print your completed will. When you are finished reading the box, click OK. You will next see the screen that enables you to review or modify any portion

of your completed will. If you wish to doublecheck your will by reading it on the screen, go to the File menu and select Preview Will.

26. To print your will, open the File menu and select Print All Documents. You will next see directions on your screen from your individual software, informing you about printing options.

27. Carefully follow the instructions that print out with your will. If a "self-proving affidavit" also prints out, ignore it for now. It helps to get your will admitted to the probate court, but it is not necessary to make a valid will, and does you no good if you are relatively young and will make a number of subsequent wills before you die. Later, if you wish, you can round up at least two of your witnesses and sign the affidavit in front of a Notary Public.

Solution 2
Unmarried
Adult children
All property to one adult individual as beneficiary
Adult children as alternates

Example
Igor Venn is 64. A widower, Igor has three grown children—who are seldom in contact with him. Igor rents an apartment which he has appointed with a valuable collection of tribal masks. He also owns an active investment portfolio and a savings account. Igor makes a will leaving his property to his sister Dorthea, and specifying the children as alternate beneficiaries if Dorthea fails to survive him.

1. Start WillMaker. If you don't know how to do this, see Section A at the beginning of this Users' Guide.

2. The first screen you will see is "Welcome to WillMaker."

3. Go to the Options menu and select Skip Info Screens. This will signal WillMaker to skip all information screens and show only screens that require you to enter information or answer questions. Then proceed with the program by clicking on Next Screen.

4. **Name**   Enter your name as you do on formal documents, first name first. When you are satisfied with your answer, click OK to move on to the next screen in the program.

5. **Social Security Number**   Enter your Social Security number if you wish. It is optional but it may help your personal representative identify your accounts and other property. Click OK.

6. **State**   Click on your state. Then click OK.

7. **County**   Enter your county as you wish it to appear in your will—such as "Caledonia County" or "County of Orange." Remember to include the word county—or its equivalent if you live in a state that uses a different term. Click OK.

8. **Are You Married**?   Click No, then OK.

9. **Children**   Click Yes, then OK.

10. **Children's Names**   Enter the full names of your children, first name first. If there is insufficient room, use middle initials or first name abbreviations. When you are satisfied that your answers are correct, click OK.

11. **Minor Children?** Click No, then OK.

12. **Children of Deceased Children?**   Click No, then OK.

13. **Specific Bequests**   Answer No; you do not wish to make specific bequests. Then click OK.

14. **Leaving Your Residuary Estate**   Enter the name of an adult individual to receive all your property as residuary beneficiary. Use the name by which he or she is commonly known. When you are satisfied with your answer, click OK.

15. **Describe Beneficiary**   Click on the button next to the top choice to indicate an individual. Click OK.

16. **If Your Residuary Beneficiary Dies Before You**   Click on the bottom button to indicate the property should go to the alternate to be named on the next screen if your first choice fails to survive you. Then click OK.

17. **Alternate Residuary Beneficiary**   Enter the names of your adult children as alternate beneficiaries. When you are satisfied that your answers are correct, click OK.

18. **Have You Named a Minor to Receive Property under Your Will?** Click on No, then click on OK.

19. **Property Management for Young Adults?** Click on No. If you would not want your adult children to receive the property without it being managed in a trust, answer Yes to this question. Then go to the Options menu, deselect Skip Info Screens, and carefully proceed through the rest of the program.

20. **Name a Personal Representative** Enter the name of one trusted adult to manage your estate—to distribute your property and pay your debts and taxes. After you are satisfied that the name is entered correctly, click OK.

21. **Alternate Personal Representative** Enter the name of your choice for alternate personal representative. Then click OK.

22. **Do You Want to Cancel Any Debts?** Click on No, then OK.

23. **Select How to Pay Debts and Expenses** Click on No, then OK.

24. **Select How to Pay Taxes** Click on No, then OK.

25. At this point, you will have entered all the information required for your will. A dialog box will appear, informing you that you can now print your completed will. When you are finished reading the box, click OK. You will next see the screen that enables you to review or modify any portion of your completed will. If you wish to doublecheck your will by reading it on the screen, go to the File menu and select Preview Will.

26. To print your will, open the File menu and select Print All Documents. You will next see directions on your screen from your individual software, informing you about printing options.

27. Carefully follow the instructions that print out with your will. If a "self-proving affidavit" also prints out, ignore it for now. It helps to get your will admitted to the probate court, but it is not necessary to make a valid will, and does you no good if you are relatively young and will make a number of subsequent wills before you die. Later, if you wish, you can round up at least two of your witnesses and sign the affidavit in front of a Notary Public.

Solution 3

Unmarried
Adult children
All property to children in equal shares
Grandchildren as alternate beneficiaries

Example

Percy Senter is 64. A widower, Percy has three grown children—to whom he is very close. He also has four grandchildren. Percy rents an apartment which he has furnished with valuable Oriental rugs. He also owns an active investment portfolio and a savings account. Percy makes a will leaving his property to his children in equal shares. In the event one or more of the children fail to survive him, Percy specifies that a deceased child's share should pass to that child's children (Percy's grandchildren).

1. Start WillMaker. If you don't know how to do this, see Section A at the beginning of this Users' Guide.

2. The first screen you will see is "Welcome to WillMaker."

3. Go to the Options menu and select Skip Info Screens. This will signal WillMaker to skip all information screens and show only screens that require you to enter information or answer questions. Then proceed with the program by clicking on Next Screen.

4. **Name**   Enter your name as you do on formal documents, first name first. When you are satisfied with your answer, click OK to move on to the next screen in the program.

5. **Social Security Number**   Enter your Social Security number if you wish. It is optional but it may help your personal representative identify your accounts and other property. Click OK.

6. **State**   Click on your state. Then click OK.

7. **County**   Enter your county as you wish it to appear in your will—such as "Caledonia County" or "County of Orange." Remember to include the word county—or its equivalent if you live in a state that uses a different term. Click OK.

8. **Are You Married**?   Click No, then OK.

9. **Children**   Click Yes, then OK.

10. **Children's Names**   Enter the full names of your children, first name first. If there is insufficient room, use middle initials or first name abbreviations. WHen you are satisfied that your answers are correct, click OK.

11. **Minor Children?** Click No, then OK.

12. **Children of Deceased Children?**   Click No, then OK.

13. **Specific Bequests**   Answer No; you do not wish to make specific bequests. Then click OK.

14. **Leaving Your Residuary Estate**   Enter the names of your adult children—using the same forms as you did earlier—to receive all your property as residuary beneficiaries. When you are satisfied that you have entered the names correctly, click OK.

15. **Describe Beneficiary**   Click on the button next to the top item for an individual, or next to the second button for two or more individuals as appropriate.

16. **If Your Residuary Beneficiary Dies Before You**   Click on the button next to the first choice to indicate that if any of your adult children named as residuary beneficiaries do not survive you, the property should go to their children—your grandchildren. Then click OK.

17. **Alternate Residuary Beneficiary**   Enter the names of one or more alternate beneficiaries to take your property if your children and their children all fail to survive you. Your choices may be relatives or friends, or a charitable institution. When you are satisfied that your answer has been entered correctly, click OK.

18. **Named Minor to Receive Property under Your Will?** Click No so that you will be routed past the screens that let you provide property management for minors.

 ### Think Twice about Management
If you named a minor as an alternate residuary beneficiary, any property he or she inherits while still a minor will have to be managed by an adult. If you do not arrange for such management in your will, the court will appoint and supervise a property guardian. Generally, the court-appointed guardian approach is not recommended.

However, using WillMaker to set up property management of minors requires some thought and a number of choices. Because your spouse is your first choice beneficiary for all your property, setting up management for the possibility that a minor will inherit is not crucial—especially for younger willmakers who are likely to live for years. However if you want to provide it, answer Y to this question. Then go to the Options menu, de-select Skip Info Screens, and carefully proceed through the rest of the program.

19. **Property Management for Young Adults?** Click on No. If you would not want your adult children to receive the property without it being managed in a trust, answer Yes to this question. Then go to the Options menu, de-select Skip Info Screens, and carefully proceed through the rest of the program.

20. **Name a Personal Representative** Enter the name of one trusted adult to manage your estate—to distribute your property and pay your debts and taxes. After you are satisfied that the name is entered correctly, click OK.

21. **Alternate Personal Representative** Enter the name of your choice for alternate personal representative. Then click OK.

22. **Do You Want to Cancel Any Debts?** Click on No, then OK.

23. **Select How to Pay Debts and Expenses** Click on No, then OK.

24. **Select How to Pay Taxes** Click on No, then OK.

25. At this point, you will have entered all the information required for your will. A dialog box will appear, informing you that you can now print your completed will. When you are finished reading the box, click OK. You will next see the screen that enables you to review or modify any portion of your completed will. If you wish to doublecheck your will by reading it on the screen, go to the File menu and select Preview Will.

26. To print your will, open the File menu and select Print all Documents. You will next see directions on your screen from your individual software, informing you about printing options.

27. Carefully follow the instructions that print out with your will. If a "self-proving affidavit" also prints out, ignore it for now. It helps to get your will admitted to the probate court, but it is not necessary to make a valid

will, and does you no good if you are relatively young and will make a number of subsequent wills before you die. Later, if you wish, you can round up at least two of your witnesses and sign the affidavit in front of a Notary Public.

Solution 4

Unmarried
Minor children
No deceased children
All property to children in equal shares
One person or charitable institution as alternate

Example

Genie McDougal is 32 and the single parent of three minor children. She rents an apartment, drives an old car and has very little property of value. Her primary concern is naming someone in her will to care for her minor children if she should die before they are grown. She writes a will leaving all her property to her children in equal shares, and naming her mother as alternate beneficiary and as personal guardian for the children.

 ### Think Twice about Management

Property left to minor children must be managed on their behalf until they become adults. These instructions bypass the WillMaker property management feature, and should only be used by you as a temporary measure or because you have little or no property to leave and are primarily interested in naming a personal guardian for your minor children. See Chapter 7 for an explanaiton of why it is important to provide property management for property left to a minor. If you want to use this structured solution but are leaving property to your minor children, remember to make a new will, when you have time, that sets up management for the property.

1. Start WillMaker. If you don't know how to do this, see Section A at the beginning of this Users' Guide.

2. The first screen you will see is "Welcome to WillMaker."

3. Go to the Options menu and select Skip Info Screens. This will signal WillMaker to skip all information screens and show only screens that require you to enter information or answer questions. Then proceed with the program by clicking on Next Screen.

4. **Name**   Enter your name as you do on formal documents, first name first. When you are satisfied with your answer, click OK to move on to the next screen in the program.

5. **Social Security Number**   Enter your Social Security number if you wish. It is optional but it may help your personal representative identify your accounts and other property. Click OK.

6. **State**   Click on your state. Then click OK.

7. **County**   Enter your county as you wish it to appear in your will—such as "Caledonia County" or "County of Orange." Remember to include the word county—or its equivalent if you live in a state that uses a different term. Click OK.

8. **Are You Married**?   Click No, then OK.

9. **Children**   Click Yes, then OK.

10. **Children's Names**   Enter the full names of your children, first name first. If there is insufficient room, use middle initials or first name abbreviations. WHen you are satisfied that your answers are correct, click OK.

11. **Minor Children?** Click on Yes, then click on OK.

12. **Children of Deceased Children?** Click on No, then OK.

13. **Specific bequests**   Click on No; you do not wish to make specific bequests. Then click OK.

14. **Leaving Your Residuary Estate**   Enter the names of your minor children—using the same form as you did earlier—to receive all your property as residuary beneficiaries. When you are satisfied the names have been answered correctly, click OK.

15. **Describe Beneficiary**   Click on the button next to the choice that describes your beneficiary.

16. **If Your Residuary Beneficiary Dies Before You**   Click on the second button. If you named more than one minor child as residuary beneficiary, the property left to a minor child who dies before you will pass to the

surviving minor children. If you named only one minor child as residuary beneficiary, the property will pass to the alternate to be named on the next screen if that child fails to survive you. Then click OK.

17. **Alternate Residuary Beneficiary**   Enter the names of one or more alternate beneficiaries to take your property if none of your minor children named as residuary beneficiaries survive you. These may be relatives or friends, or a charitable institution. When you are satisfied the names are entered properly, click OK.

18. **Personal Guardian**   Enter the name of a close relative or friend to be personal guardian of your minor children in case you and the other parent cannot care for the child. When you have entered the answers correctly, click OK.

19. **Alternate Personal Guardian**   Enter the name of an alternate personal guardian—perhaps the spouse of the person you named as your first choice. If you don't want to name an alternate, click OK without making an entry first.

20. **Have You Named a Minor to Receive Property under Your Will?** Click on No so that you will be routed past the screens that let you provide property management for minors. But heed the caution set out earlier in this set of instructions. Property management for minor children is highly recommended. Only if you have little property and your main concern is naming a guardian for your minor children should you forego the WillMaker property management options. If you do decide to use them for property you are leaving to your minor children, answer Yes to this question. Then go to the Options menu, de-select Skip Info Screens, and carefully proceed through the rest of the program.

21. **Property Management for Young Adults?** Click on No, then OK.

22. **Name a Personal Representative**   Enter the name of one trusted adult to manage your estate—to distribute your property and pay your debts and taxes. After you are satisfied that the name is entered correctly, click OK.

23. **Alternate Personal Representative**   Enter the name of your choice for alternate personal representative. Then click OK.

24. **Do You Want to Cancel Any Debts?** Click on No, then OK.

23. **Select How to Pay Debts and Expenses**   Click on No, then OK.

25. **Select How to Pay Taxes**   Click on No, then OK.

26. At this point, you will have entered all the information required for your will. A dialog box will appear, informing you that you can now print your completed will. When you are finished reading the box, click OK. You will next see the screen that enables you to review or modify any portion of your completed will. If you wish to doublecheck your will by reading it on the screen, go to the File menu and select Preview Will.

27. To print your will, open the File menu and select Print All Documents. You will next see directions on your screen from your individual software, informing you about printing options.

28. Carefully follow the instructions that print out with your will. If a "self-proving affidavit" also prints out, ignore it for now. It helps to get your will admitted to the probate court, but it is not necessary to make a valid will, and does you no good if you are relatively young and will make a number of subsequent wills before you die. Later, if you wish, you can round up at least two of your witnesses and sign the affidavit in front of a Notary Public.

7 Caring for Children and Their Property

Becoming a parent is what may have motivated you to buckle down to the task of writing your will. Although contemplating the possibility of your early death can be wrenching, it is important to face up to it and adopt the best contingent plan for the care of your young children. If the other parent is available, then he or she can handle the task. But life is full of possibilities—some of them rather bleak. You and the other parent might die close together in time. Or you may currently be a single parent, and need to come to terms with what will happen if you do not survive until the children become adults.

When planning for the possibility of your early death, you should consider:

• who will care for your minor children; and

• who will manage property you leave them.

WillMaker lets you make these decisions separately. This gives you the opportunity to place these responsibilities in the hands of the same person, or if need be, different people.

If your minor children may inherit valuable property from you, you must face another issue. Except for items of little value, minors are not permitted by law to have control over property. Instead, that property will have to be managed by a responsible adult. It is of vital importance to your children's interests that you arrange for this management yourself, in your will, rather than leave it up to a court to appoint and supervise a property manager. WillMaker lets you establish management for property left to a minor—and that management can last until the minor turns an age you choose, up to and including 35.

It also makes good sense to establish management for property you plan to leave to other minor children—your grandchildren, nieces and nephews. That way, you free their parents, or other adults responsible for them, from the expensive and time-consuming burden of having to go to court to get legal authority to manage the property on behalf of the minor. Here, too, you can use WillMaker to provide property management that lasts until the young beneficiary is 35 years old.

And those considering young adults as beneficiaries may also want distribution of inherited property deferred until a later age. As with minors, you can use WillMaker to defer distribution of property left to any young adult—yours or someone else's—until the beneficiary reaches an age you choose, up to and including 35.

Explaining Your Bequests to Your Children

WillMaker, of course, allows you to divide up your property among your children as you see fit. If your children are already responsible adults, your prime concern will likely be about fairness—given the circumstances and the children's needs. Often, this will mean dividing your property equally among your children. Sometimes, however, the special health or educational needs of one child, the relative affluence and stability of another or the fact that you are estranged from a child will be the impetus for you to make an uneven distribution.

Doing this can sometimes raise serious worries—a child who receives less property may conclude that you cared for him or her less. To deal with this, you may wish to explain your reasons for dividing your property unequally. Because of the risk of adding illegal or confusing language, WillMaker does not allow you to make this explanation in your will. Fortunately, there is a sound and sensible way to express your reasons and feelings. Simply prepare a separate letter to accompany your will. (See Chapter 12, Section A for a sample letter.)

A. Identify Your Children in Your Will

It is important to name all your children when making your WillMaker will. This warning is backed by strong legal reasoning: If a minor or adult child is neither named in a will nor specifically disinherited, the law of most states assumes that you accidentally forgot to include that child. The effect is that the overlooked child has a right to the same share of your estate he or she would be entitled to had you left no will. This amount varies from state to state, often depending on your family composition, but would likely be a significant percentage of your property.

These laws are intended to protect both the interests of the accidentally forgotten child—termed a "pretermitted heir"—and the person making the will. This rule applies no matter how old your children are when you die—and no matter whether you specifically plan to leave them any property in your will.

Example

Bruno leaves nothing to his daughter Portia in his will because they have been estranged for years. He neither names her nor specifically disinherits her. When Bruno dies, Portia is 66 years old. Portia is entitled to sue for a share of Bruno's estate as a pretermitted heir.

WillMaker protects you against the pretermitted heir rule by asking you to name all your children and then automatically leaving each child $1. Some states require that children must also be left something in the will as well as being named in it to avoid the pretermitted heir rule. Since all children will be named and provided for in your WillMaker will, none of them will qualify as accidentally forgotten—or pretermitted—heirs. You will probably want to give each or most of your children more than $1. And you can. Leave each child any property you wish—real estate, personal property, cash—using one of the specific bequest screens or as part of your residuary estate. (See Chapter 5 for details about leaving property to your beneficiaries, and Section D of this chapter about providing management for property left to minor or young adults).

To be sure this system of leaving $1 to each child protects you, when WillMaker asks for your children, name all of them, including:

- children born to or adopted by you while you were married to your current spouse;

- children born to or adopted by you when you were married to a previous spouse;

- children born to or adopted by you when you were not married; and

- children born to you but then adopted by someone else.[1]

It is unnecessary to name unadopted stepchildren here, but you may provide for them however you wish in your will.

To list your children, enter their full names in the sequence and format you want the names to appear in your will.

---

[1]Under the law in most states, you have no legal relationship with these children, and therefore, they would not be considered pretermitted heirs. However, if you have any doubt about whether the adoption was legal or final, name these children in your WillMaker will.

Example

Peter John Jones, Sophie Elizabeth Jones and Harold Portnoy Jones.

There should be enough room on the screen to list all your children in this manner. If, however, you have many children and they have long names, causing space problems, identify them by eliminating their middle names—or listing all their first names and then putting the common last name at the end of the sequence.

Example

Peter, Sophie, Harold, Rubin, Julian, Stanley, Robert, Ralph, Jennifer and Jill Jones.

 Don't Use "All My Children"

Some people want to skip naming their children individually and put in "all my children," "my surviving children," "my lawful heirs," or "my issue." Don't do it. It can be confusing and may lead to pretermitted heir problems down the line.

B. Identify Children of a Deceased Child

WillMaker asks you to name the children of a deceased child. Name all such grandchildren—including children your child legally adopted and those born while he or she was not married.

This question is asked because the rule that allows overlooked or "pretermitted" children to sue to get a share of your estate also applies to grandchildren you may have overlooked in your will if their parent (your child) is dead.

As it does for your own children, WillMaker automatically leaves each grandchild whose parent is deceased $1—and therefore eliminates the problem. Again, you are free to leave the grandchild additional property if you choose.

▶ **Keep Your Will Up-To-Date**
▶
▶ The WillMaker system of naming all your children and leaving each $1 requires
▶ that you make a new will in the following two situations:
▶ • If a child is born to or legally adopted by you after you make your will. You
▶   must change your will to list the new child. If you do not, that child may
▶   challenge your will as a pretermitted heir and sue to receive a share of what
▶   you leave.
▶ • If one of your children dies before you do and leaves children of his or her
▶   own. The laws of many states require that you name and provide for the
▶   children of deceased children. If you do not, they are considered pretermitted
▶   heirs. To protect against this, make a new will, naming these grandchildren so
▶   that they will receive at least $1.
▶ (See Chapter 11 for information on how to keep your will up-to-date.)

C. Name a Guardian for Your Minor Children

This section discusses using WillMaker to choose a personal guardian to care for the children's basic health, education and other daily needs.

1. Why Name a Personal Guardian?

Among the most pressing concerns of parents with minor children is who will care for the children if one or both of them die before the children reach 18. The general legal rule: If there are two parents willing and able to care for the children, and one dies, the other will take over physical custody and responsibility for caring for the child. In many states, the surviving parent may also be given authority by a court to manage any property the deceased parent left to the children—unless the deceased parent has specified a different property management arrangement in a will.

But what if both parents of a minor child die, or in the case of a single parent, there is not another parent able or willing to do the job? Using WillMaker, you can tackle these concerns by naming a personal guardian and an alternate. The person you name will normally be appointed by the court to act as a surrogate parent for your minor children if:

- there is no surviving natural or adoptive parent able to properly care for the children; and

- the court agrees that your choice is in the best interests of the children.

If both parents are making their wills, they should name the same person as guardian—to avoid the possibility of a dispute and perhaps even a court battle should they die simultaneously. But remember, if one spouse dies first, the other will almost always assume custody and will then be free to make a new will naming a different personal guardian if he or she wishes. In short, in a family where both parents are active caretakers, the personal guardian named in a will cares for the children only if both parents die at the same time or close together.

WillMaker allows only one person to be named as personal guardian and one person as alternate personal guardian for all of a parent's minor children. While it is legally permissible to name co-guardians, it is normally a poor idea because of the possibility that the co-guardians will later disagree or go separate ways.

2. Choosing a Personal Guardian

To qualify as a personal guardian, your choice must be an adult—18 in most states—and competent to do the job. For obvious reasons, you should first consider an adult with whom the child already has a close relationship—a stepparent, grandparent, aunt or uncle, older sibling, close friend of the family or even a neighbor. But, whoever you choose, be sure that person is mature, goodhearted and willing and able to assume the responsibility.

3. Choosing an Alternate Personal Guardian

WillMaker lets you name a "back-up" or alternate personal guardian to serve
in case your first choice either changes his or her mind or is unable to do the
job at your death. The considerations involved in naming an alternate personal
guardian are the same as those you considered when making your first choice:
maturity, a good heart, familiarity with the children and willingness to serve.

4. Explaining Your Choice for Guardian

If you are separated or divorced, you may have strong ideas about why the
child's other parent, or perhaps a grandparent, should not have custody of
your minor children. In an age when many parents live separately, the
following predicaments are sadly common:

"I have custody of my three children. I don't want my ex-husband, who I
believe is emotionally destructive, to get custody of our children if I die. Can I
choose a guardian to serve instead of him?"

"I have legal custody of my daughter and I've remarried. My present wife
is a much better mother to my daughter than my ex-wife, who never cared for
her properly. What can I do to make sure my present wife gets custody if I
die?"

"I live with a man who's been a good parent to my children for six years.
My father doesn't like the fact that we aren't married and may well try to get
custody of the kids if I die. What can I do to see that my mate gets custody?"

There is no definitive answer to these questions. If you die while the child
is still a minor and the other parent disputes your choice in court, the judge
will likely grant custody to the other natural parent, unless this parent:

• has legally abandoned the child by not providing for or visiting the child
  for an extended period; or

• is clearly unfit as a parent.

It is usually difficult to prove that a parent is unfit, absent serious and
obvious problems such as chronic drug or alcohol abuse, mental illness, or a
history of child abuse. The fact that you do not like or respect the other parent

is never enough, by itself, for a court to deny custody to him or her. But if you honestly believe the other natural parent is incapable of caring for your children properly, or simply will not assume the responsibility, here's how to proceed:

Step 1

In your will, name the person you want to be your child's personal guardian.

Example

Susan and Fred, an unmarried couple, have two minor children. Although Susan loves Fred, she does not think he is capable of raising the children on his own. She uses WillMaker to name her mother, Elinor, as guardian. If Susan later dies, Fred, as the children's natural parent, will be given first priority over Elinor, despite Susan's will, assuming the court finds he is willing and able to care for the children. However, if the court finds that Fred should not be personal guardian, Elinor would get the nod, assuming she was fit.

Example

Susan and Fred live together with Susan's minor children from an earlier marriage. The natural father is out of the picture, but Susan fears that her mother, Elinor, who does not approve of unmarried couples living together, will try to get custody of the kids if something happens to her. Susan wants Fred to have custody because he knows the children well and loves them. She can use WillMaker to name Fred as personal guardian and attach a separate letter to her will making the reasons for this choice clear. (See Step 2, below.) If Susan dies and Elinor goes to court to get custody, the fact that she named Fred will give him a big advantage. If he is a good parent, he is likely to get custody in most states.

Step 2

Explain in a letter that you attach to your will the reasons for making your choice. (See Chapter 12, Section A for a sample letter that you can modify to suit your circumstances.)

▶
▶ **Custody Difficulties for Lesbians and Gay Men**
▶ Many lesbians and gay men have been married and have become parents. If only
▶ one of the couple is a lesbian or gay, and there is later an acrimonious divorce,
▶ who gets custody of the children often involves a difficult legal battle. In a court
▶ fight over custody, judges are supposed to consider all factors and arrive at a
▶ decision in the "best interests of the child." This means that virtually any
▶ information about a parent's lifestyle, sexual identity and behavior can be brought
▶ out in court. In many states, especially in the south and midwest, evidence of a
▶ parent's lesbian or gay sexual identity is still legally accepted reason for denying
▶ custody.[2]

D. Property Management: An Overview

WillMaker allows you to think ahead and establish management for property you leave in your will to any beneficiaries who may be minors or young adults when you die. Management established under WillMaker may last until an age you choose—up to and including age 35.

This section presents an overview of basic property management considerations. Section E discusses how to use WillMaker to put your management choices into your will.

Property management consists of naming a trusted adult to be in charge of caring for and accurately accounting for the property a young beneficiary inherits under your will until the beneficiary turns a specific age. The property being managed for the young beneficiary must be held, invested or spent in

---

[2]If you anticipate a contested custody case, you will find guidance in *A Legal Guide for Lesbian and Gay Couples*, by Hayden Curry and Denis Clifford (Nolo Press).

the best interest of the beneficiary. In other words, someone other than the young beneficiary will decide if their inheritance will be spent on college tuition or a new sports car.

1. Property Management for Minors—Generally

Except for property of little value—usually under $1,000—minors may not directly control property they inherit under a will. The property must be managed by an adult for the minor's benefit until he or she turns 18. If you do not provide this management in your will, the court will do it for you—an expensive, public and time-consuming alternative requiring court supervision of how the guardian manages and spends the money.

In addition, you may want to provide that management for property left to a minor continues beyond age 18—the age at which a guardianship ends. WillMaker allows this management to last up to and including age 35.

2. Property Management for Young Adults—Generally

If you are leaving valuable property to someone who is in his or her late teens or early twenties, you may justifiably wish to delay the time the young beneficiary actually gets to use and control it. WillMaker lets you extend the time property left to young adults is managed until they reach an age up to and including 35.

3. Leaving Property to Your Own Minor Children

If you are married, you may choose to leave your property directly to your spouse and trust him or her to use good judgment in providing for your children's current and future needs. Even if you do this, however, you are not necessarily freed from the need to provide property management. To plan for the possibility that your spouse dies close in time to you, you may want to name your children as alternate beneficiaries. And then you will want to appoint a trusted adult as manager for the property they could inherit.

Finally, once you choose a person to manage the property, you must decide what you want to happen when your children reach the age of 18. You can choose to have the property left them handed over in one lump sum, or instead have the property management continued until the children are somewhat older.

4. Property Management for the Children of Others

If it is possible that other people's children—such as your grandchildren—will take property under your will, you must also address how and whether this property is to be managed. This is important. If the child is a minor and you do not provide management for the property, the child's parent will usually be required to establish a time-consuming and relatively expensive court-supervised property guardianship. It is much wiser to use WillMaker to name the child's parent or some other person or institution as property manager.

▶ What Happens If the Minor Does Not Inherit Property

If you arrange for property management for a minor, but the minor never inherits the property, no harm is done. The management provisions for that minor are ignored. For instance, suppose you identify a favorite niece to take property as an alternate beneficiary, and provide management for that property until the niece turns 25. If the niece fails to get the property because your first choice beneficiary survives you, no property management will be established for her, since none will be needed.

E. Property Management Under WillMaker

WillMaker offers two basic legal approaches to property management for minors and young adults:

1. The Uniform Transfers to Minors Act

The Uniform Transfers to Minors Act (UTMA) is one of a number of uniform laws in effect in many states.[3] It allows you to name a "custodian" to manage property you leave to a minor. The management ends when the minor reaches age 18 to 25, depending on state law.

States are free to adopt or reject the UTMA, which is a "model law" proposed by a group of legal scholars who make up the Uniform Law Commission. So far, over half the states have adopted the UTMA—many making minor changes to it. There is every reason to believe that the UTMA will be universally adopted, but that will take a few more years. Since adoption means that it is built into the legal framework, if the UTMA is already on the books in your state, all banks, insurance companies, brokers and other financial institutions should already be familiar with it.

▶
▶
▶ **States That Have Not Adopted the UTMA**
▶
▶ At present, the UTMA has not been adopted in these states: Connecticut,
▶ Delaware, Michigan, Mississippi, Nebraska, New York, Pennsylvania, South
▶ Carolina, Tennessee, Texas, and Vermont.
▶
▶   If you are a resident of one of the states, don't worry. You can set up property
▶ management for any minor or young adult beneficiary using the WillMaker
▶ children's trust, discussed in Section 2, below.

If the UTMA has been adopted in your state, you may use it to specify a custodian to manage property you leave a minor in your will until the age at which the laws of your state require that it be turned over to the minor. Depending on your state, this varies from 18 to 21; California allows you to extend management until 25. The WillMaker program keeps track of the state you indicate as your residence and tells you whether the UTMA is available, and if so, the age at which property management under it must end.

---

[3]The UTMA was written to supplement an earlier uniform act—the Uniform Gifts to Minors Act (UGMA)—which had been adopted by all states. The UGMA only applies to gifts made by living people and only applies to personal property. The UTMA, on the other hand, allows the creation of management for both real and personal property transferred to minors in a will or living trust as well as by gift.

► **Age Limits for Property Management in UTMA States**

► Property Management Must End at Age 18 in:

►   District of Columbia, Kentucky, Nevada, Oklahoma,

►   Rhode Island and South Dakota

► Property Management Must End at an Age You Choose Between Age 18 and 21 in:

►   Arkansas, Maine, New Jersey, North Carolina and Virginia

► Property Management Must End at Age 21 in:

►   Alabama, Arizona, Colorado, Florida, Georgia, Hawaii, Idaho, Illinois, Indiana,

►   Iowa, Kansas, Maryland, Massachusetts, Minnesota, Missouri, Montana, New

►   Hampshire, New Mexico, North Dakota, Ohio, Oregon, Utah, Washington,

►   West Virginia, Wisconsin and Wyoming

► Property Management Must End by Age 25 in:

►   Alaska and California

Among the powers the UTMA gives the custodian are the right, without court approval, "to collect, hold, manage, invest and reinvest" the property, and to spend "as much of the custodial property as the custodian considers advisable for the use and benefit of the minor." The custodian must also keep records so that tax returns can be filed on behalf of the minor and must otherwise act as a prudent person would when in control of another's property.

► **Life Insurance Note**

► Often the major source of property left to children comes from a life insurance
► policy naming the children as beneficiaries. If you want the insurance proceeds for
► a particular child to be managed, and you live in a state that has adopted the
► UTMA, instruct your insurance agent to provide you with the form necessary to
► name a custodian to manage the property for the beneficiary under the terms of
► this Act.

2. The WillMaker Children's Trust

The WillMaker children's trust, which can be used in all states, is a legal structure you establish in your will. If you create a trust, any property inherited by a minor beneficiary will be managed by a person or institution you choose to serve as trustee until the beneficiary turns an age you choose—through age 35. The trustee's powers are listed in your will. The trustee may use trust assets for the education, medical needs and living expenses of the minor or young adult beneficiary. All property you leave to a beneficiary for whom a trust is established will be managed under the terms of the trust.

Because management under the WillMaker children's trust can be extended through age 35, it is also suitable to use for property left to young adults. (The pros and cons of the two management options are discussed in Section 3, below.)

Property Management Needs Not Covered by WillMaker

The property management features offered by WillMaker—the UTMA and children's trust—are similar and provide the property manager with broad management authority adequate for most minors and young adults. However, they are not designed to:

- provide skilled long-term management of a business according to specific guidelines;

- provide for management of funds beyond age 35 for a person with spendthrift tendencies or other personal habits that may impede sound financial management beyond young adulthood; or

- meet a disadvantaged beneficiary's special needs. A physical, mental or developmental disability will likely require management customized to the beneficiary's circumstances, both to perpetuate the beneficiary's way of life and to preserve the property, while assuring that the beneficiary continues to qualify for government benefits.

For all these situations, specific trust provisions custom-tailored to the needs of the beneficiary and your wishes should be drafted by an attorney experienced in this type of work.

3. Should You Use the UTMA or WillMaker Children's Trust?

For each minor or young adult to whom you leave property, you must decide which management approach to use—the UTMA or the children's trust. Because both are safe, efficient and easy to put in place, either can be used

for many situations. This section helps you decide which is best for you and
yours.

▶ When to Use the UTMA

As a general rule, the less valuable the property involved and the more mature the
child, the more appropriate the UTMA is because it is simpler to use than the
children's trust. There are a couple of reasons for this.

Because the UTMA is built into state law, financial institutions know about it
and should make it easy for the custodian to carry out property management
duties. To set up a children's trust, the financial institution would have to be given
a copy of the trust document and may tie up the proceeding in red tape to be sure
the trustee is acting under its terms.

Also, a custodian acting under the UTMA need not file a separate income tax
return for the property being managed; it can be included in the young
beneficiary's return. However, with a children's trust, both the beneficiary and the
trust must file returns.

Because the UTMA requires termination of the management at a relatively
young age, if the property you are leaving is worth $50,000 or less—or the child is
likely to be able to handle more than that by age 21 (25 in California), use the
UTMA. After all, $50,000 is likely to be used up long before management under the
UTMA ends—at least in most states.

> ### When to Use the WillMaker Children's Trust
>
> As a general rule, the more property is worth, and the less mature the young beneficiary, the better it is to use the children's trust, even though doing so is a bit more work for the property manager than using the UTMA. For example, if a minor or young adult stands to inherit a fairly large amount of property—such as $200,000 or more—you might not want it all distributed by your state's UTMA cut-off age, which is usually 18 or 21. In such circumstances, you will be better off using the WillMaker children's trust.

Remember, under the children's trust, management can last until an age you choose—up to and including 35.

F. Choosing a Property Manager

You may name one person and one successor, who will take over if your first choice is unable to serve, to manage the property. If you use the UTMA, these people will be called the custodian and successor custodian. If you use the WillMaker children's trust, they will be called the trustee and successor trustee.

> ### Selecting an Institution as Property Manager
>
> If you are using the UTMA, you must name a person as custodian—you cannot name an institution. The WillMaker children's trust, however, allows an institution to serve as trustee. Still, it is rarely a good idea to pick a bank or other institution as trustee. Most banks will not accept a trust with less than $200,000 worth of liquid assets.[4] When they do agree to take a trust, they charge large management and administrative fees. All trustees are entitled to reasonable compensation for their services—paid from trust assets. But family members or close friends often waive payments or accept far less than banks when chosen to act as trustee. If you cannot find an individual you think is suitable for handling your assets and do not have enough property to be managed by a financial institution, you may be better off not creating a trust.

---

[4]It is common for banks to manage the assets of all trusts worth less than $1,000,000 as part of one large fund, while charging fees as if they were individually managed. Any trustee who invests trust money in a conservatively-run mutual fund can normally do at least as well at a fraction of the cost.

Choosing someone to manage your children's finances is almost as important a decision as choosing someone to take custody of them after your death. Name someone you trust, who is familiar with managing the kind of assets you leave to your children, and who shares your attitudes and values about how the money should be spent.

As a general rule, your choice for custodian or trustee should also live in or near to the state where the property will be managed.[5]

And you need not worry about finding a financial wizard to be your property manager. Under both the UTMA and the WillMaker children's trust, the property manager—custodian or trustee—has the power to hire professionals to prepare accountings and tax returns and to give investment advice. Anyone hired for such help may be paid out of the property being managed. The custodian or trustee's main jobs are to manage the property honestly, make basic decisions about how to take care of the assets wisely and sensibly mete out the money to the trust beneficiary.

Whoever you choose as custodian or trustee, it is essential to get his or her consent first. This will also give you a chance to discuss, in general terms, how you would like the property to be managed to be sure the manager you select agrees with your vision and fully understands the beneficiary's needs.

---

[5]Some states require trustees to live in the state where the trust is created. If you are using the trust option and wish to select a trustee who lives in a different state than you do, try to select an in-state person as the successor trustee. Then, if your first choice is prevented by the law of your state from serving, the alternate trustee will be able to step in and do the job.

Example

Ralph and Ariadne agree that Ariadne's sister, Penny, should be guardian of their kids should they both die, but that the $100,000 worth of stock the three kids will inherit might better be handled by someone with more business experience and who will be better able to resist the children's urgings to spend the money frivolously. In each of their wills, they name Penny as personal guardian of the children, but also create trusts for the property they are leaving to their children. They name each other as trustees, and Ralph's mother, Phyllis, who has investment and business knowledge and lots of experience in handling headstrong adolescents, as the alternate trustee, after obtaining her consent. Ralph and Ariadne also decide that one of their children, who is somewhat immature, should receive his share of the estate—at least the portion not already disbursed for his benefit by the trustee—upon turning 25, and the other two children should get their shares when they turn 21.

▶ General Rules for Naming a Property Manager

Here are a few general principles to follow when choosing a property manager.

- It is usually preferable to combine the personal care and property management functions for a particular minor child in the hands of one person. Think first who is likely to be caring for the children if you die, and then consider if that person is also a good choice for property manager. If you must name two different people, try to choose people who get along well; they will have to work together.

- If you believe that the person who will be caring for the minor is not the best person to handle the minor's finances, consider an adult who is capable and is willing to serve.

- If you are married and leaving property directly to your minor children, consider naming your spouse as first choice as property manager.

- For property being left to young adults, select an honest person with business savvy to manage the property.

G. Choosing an Age to Terminate Management

For management under the UTMA, the age at which management terminates is seldom an issue. In all but a few states, the management terminates automatically at age 18 or 21, depending on the state; in California, it can be from 21 to 25. (See Section E3, above.)

Under the WillMaker children's trust, however, you may select any age up to 35 for the management to terminate. There is no general rule that will direct you in choosing an age for a particular beneficiary to get whatever trust property has not been spent on the beneficiary's health, welfare and educational needs. That will depend on:

- the amount of money involved;

- how much control you would like to impose over it;

- the beneficiary's likely level of maturity as a young adult. For small children, this may be difficult to predict, but by the time most youngsters reach their teens, you should have a pretty good indication; and

- whether the property you leave, such as rental property or a small business, needs sophisticated management that a young beneficiary is unlikely to master.

H. Examples of Choosing Property Management Options

Here are some examples of how the WillMaker property management options might be selected. The following scenarios are only intended as suggestions. Remember, if you live in a state that has not adopted the UTMA, your only property management option is the WillMaker children's trust.

Example 1
Married
Adult children age 25 and older

You want to leave all your property, worth $150,000, to your spouse and name surviving children as alternate beneficiaries. As long as you think the children are all sufficiently mature to handle their share of the property if your spouse fails to survive you, answer no when WillMaker asks if you wish to set up property management.

Example 2

Married
Children aged 19, 21 and 23

You want to leave all your property, which is worth $300,000, to your spouse and name your surviving children as alternate beneficiaries. You sensibly opt for property management in case the children get the property—if you and your spouse both die— and establish a children's trust for each child, to end at age 30. You name your financially experienced brother as trustee. You can leave each of the children the same amount of property, or you can leave varying amounts. You would not want to use the UTMA even if available in your state because it requires that property management end at age 21 (25 in California).

Example 3

Married
Children aged 2, 5 and 9

You want to leave all your property, which is worth $150,000, to your spouse and name your children as alternate beneficiaries. You use the property management feature and select the UTMA option (if your state offers it) for all property each child inherits under your will. You name your wife's mother—the same person you have named as personal guardian—as custodian, and name your brother as alternate guardian and successor custodian. The property will be managed by the custodian until the age allowed under the UTMA—18, 21, or 25, depending on the state.

Later, when your children are older and you have accumulated more property, you may wish to make a new will and switch from the UTMA approach to the children's trust, to extend the age of management until a later age (up to age 35) for one or more of the children. Also, you may wish to name different property managers for each child.

Alternative If you are in a state that has not adopted the UTMA, use the trust option and set the distribution ages to a later time than permitted by the UTMA.

Example 4

Single or married

Two minor children from a previous marriage and one minor child
   with your present partner

You want to leave all your property, which is worth $150,000, directly to your children.
You can use either the UTMA or the trust for each child, and name separate custodians
or trustees, if you wish.

 If you are married, your spouse has a right to claim a portion of your
property, so it is usually unwise to leave it all to your children unless
your spouse agrees with that plan. (See Chapter 4, Section C.)

Example 5

Single or married

Two adult children from a previous marriage—ages 23 and 27—and one minor child
   with your present partner

You decide to divide $300,000 equally among the children. To accomplish this, you
establish a trust for each child from the previous marriage and put the termination age
at 30. You name your current spouse, who gets along well with the children, as trustee
and a local trust company as alternate trustee. Because your third child is an unusually
mature teenager, you choose the UTMA for this child and select 21 as the age at which
this child takes any remaining property outright. You appoint your wife as custodian
and the trust company as successor custodian.

Example 6

Married or single

One daughter of your own, age 32, and three minor grandchildren

You want to leave $50,000 directly to each of the grandchildren. You establish a
custodianship under the UTMA for each grandchild, and name your daughter as
custodian and her husband as successor custodian.

8 Choosing a Personal Representative (Executor)

Using WillMaker, you can name a personal representative—also called an executor. Your personal representative will have legal responsibility, after your death, for safeguarding and handling your property, seeing that debts and taxes are paid and distributing what is left to your beneficiaries as your will directs.

A. Duties of a Personal Representative

Depending on the amount of property involved and the complexity of the plans for it, serving as a personal representative is a job that can be fairly easy or require a good deal of time and patience.

▶
▶
▶ ### Make Your Will and Records Accessible
▶
▶ As the willmaker, you can help with the personal representative's first task:
▶ locating your will. Keep a copy in a fairly obvious place—a desk, file cabinet, safe
▶ deposit box. And make sure your personal representative has access to it.
▶
▶ Should you need help in getting organized, *For the Record* by Carol Pladsen
▶ and Ralph Warner (Nolo Press) is an easy-to-use software program that provides a
▶ single place to keep a complete inventory of all your legal, financial and personal
▶ records. It also offers an overview of how to reduce estate taxes and avoid
▶ probate.

Your personal representative will have a number of other duties—some of
which may require the help of an accountant or other professional. If someone
else must be hired to assist, he or she may be paid from the estate.

Most of the personal representative's tasks are not inherently difficult; they
just demand good organizational skills, perseverance and a little business
savvy.

Typically, the personal representative must:

- obtain certified copies of the death certificate;

- locate will beneficiaries;

- examine and inventory the deceased person's safety deposit boxes;

- collect the deceased person's mail;

- cancel credit cards and subscriptions;

- notify Social Security and other benefit plan administrators of the death;

- learn about the deceased person's property—which may involve examining
  bankbooks, deeds, insurance policies, tax returns and many other records;

- get bank accounts released or, in the case of pay-on-death accounts, get
  them transferred to their new owner;

- collect any death benefits from life insurance policies, Social Security,
  veterans' benefits and other benefits due from the deceased's union,
  fraternal society or employer;

- except for very small estates, file papers to begin the probate of the
  deceased's estate. This involves transferring property and making sure the
  deceased's final debts and taxes are paid;

- prepare final income tax forms for the deceased, and if necessary, file estate tax returns for the estate; and

- handle the probate process, or hire a lawyer to do so. A personal representative who goes it alone will have to file papers and the will with the probate court—and may need to make a brief appearance or two in court.

    While many people name a spouse, close relative or other beneficiary who may choose not to be paid for the task, a personal representative is legally entitled to a fee for his or her services, usually payable from the estate. The fee scale varies from state to state, but ranges from a fixed percentage of the value of your property at death to the more amorphous "reasonable compensation" usually determined by a local probate court. Either way, these fees typically amount to several percent of the estate's value.

B. Naming a Personal Representative

Glancing through the list of the personal representative's duties in Section A above should help tip you off about who you know that might be the best person for the job: the prime characteristics are being organized, being good with details and being honest. Obviously, for many tasks, such as collecting mail and finding important records and papers, it is most helpful to name someone who lives nearby and who is familiar with your business affairs.

1. Criteria for Choosing a Personal Representative

The most important guideline in naming a personal representative is to choose someone you trust and who you don't mind having access to your personal records and finances after your death. Many people choose someone who is also named to inherit a substantial amount of property under their will. This makes sense because a person with an interest in how your property is distributed—a spouse, mate, child, or close family member—is also likely to do a conscientious job as personal representative. And he or she will probably also come equipped with knowledge of where your records are kept and an understanding of why you want your property split up as you have directed.

But whoever you select, make sure the person is willing to do the job. Discuss the job with your choice before naming him or her in your will.

While it is almost always best to choose a trusted person for the job, you may not know anyone who is up to the task—especially if your estate is large and complicated and your beneficiaries are very old, very young, or just inexperienced in financial matters. If so, you can select a trust management firm to act as your personal representative. If that is your leaning, first be sure the institution you choose is willing to act. Most will not accept the job unless your estate is fairly large—worth at least $250,000 and often more. Also, understand that institutions charge a hefty fee for acting as personal representative—usually both a percentage of the value of property to be managed and a number of smaller fees for routine services such as buying and selling property.

You Cannot Name Two to Share the Job

WillMaker requires you to name only one person or institution as personal representative. This avoids the problems that often result if the two people named to act together cannot agree on the decisions to be made—or if one of them dies or otherwise becomes unable to act.

2. If You Do Not Name a Personal Representative

If for some reason you do not name a personal representative in your will, the document will still be valid as a will. But your decision will not have been a wise one. It will most often mean that a court will have to scurry and scrounge to come up with a willing relative to serve. If that fails, the court will probably appoint someone to do the job who is likely to be unfamiliar with you, your property and your beneficiaries. People appointed by the court to serve are called administrators.

But sometimes, a person making a will fails to name a personal representative—or names someone who has since died or cannot serve. The laws in many states provide that anyone who is entitled under the will to take over half a person's property has first priority to serve as personal representative. If no such person is apparent, courts will generally look for someone to serve among the following groups of people, in the following priority:

Surviving spouse
Children
Grandchildren
Greatgrandchildren
Parents
Brothers and sisters
Grandparents
Uncles, aunts, first cousins
Children of deceased spouse
Other next of kin
Relatives of a deceased spouse
Conservator or guardian
Public administrator
Creditors
Any other person

C. Naming an Alternate Personal Representative

In case you name someone to serve as executor who dies before you do or for any other reason is unwilling or unable to take on the responsibilities, you should name an alternate to serve instead.

In choosing an alternate personal representative, consider the same factors you did in naming your first choice.

9 Planning to Pay Debts and Expenses

▶
▶ **When Planning to Pay Debts and Death Taxes Isn't Needed**
▶ You need be concerned about how to cover your debts and death taxes only
▶ when your willmaking plan involves dividing up your property among a number
▶ of beneficiaries.
▶   If you plan to leave all of your property to your spouse, or equally to two or
▶ more people without specifying what property goes to which person, there is no
▶ real need to plan how your debts, expenses and death taxes should be paid. Your
▶ spouse or the co-beneficiaries should be able to agree with your personal
▶ representative—who will likely be one of these people—as to which of your assets
▶ should be used.

A. Liabilities of Your Estate

If you live owing money, chances are you'll die owing money. If you do, your
personal representative will be responsible for rounding up your property and
making sure all your outstanding debts are satisfied before any of the property
is put in the hands of those you have named to get it. Your estate will be
liable for:

- **Debts you owe when you die—personal loans, credit card bills, mortgage loans, income taxes** Whether such debts pass to the beneficiary along with the property, or must be paid out of the estate depends upon how the debt is characterized. (See Section B.)

- **Expenses incurred after your death—costs of funeral, burial and probate** Probate and estate administration fees typically run about 5% to 7% of the value of the property you leave in your will. Unless you specify otherwise, the fees will be paid according to the law of your state. Typically, this means they come from your residuary estate. This may mean your residuary beneficiary will receive less than you intended, especially if you have relied on your residuary clause to pass most of your estate.

- **Death taxes** If your net estate is more than $600,000 at death, it will likely owe federal estate taxes. It may also owe state death taxes; some states tax estates and some do not. (See Chapter 13, Section E, for a list.) Unless you specify otherwise in your will, the taxes will normally be paid proportionately out of the estate's liquid assets. This means that beneficiary's property will be reduced by the percentage that the property bears to the total liquid assets. Liquid assets include bank accounts, money market accounts and marketable securities. Real estate and tangible personal property such as cars, furniture and antiques are excluded. This could cause a problem if, for example, you left your bank account with $50,000 in it to a favorite nephew and your death tax liability—most of which resulted from valuable real property left to another beneficiary—gobbled up all or most of it.

B. Understanding Debts and Expenses of Probate

There are two basic kinds of debts with which you need be concerned when making a will—"secured" and "unsecured."

1. Secured Debts

As used here, secured debts are any debts owed on specific property that must be paid before title to that property fully belongs to its owner.

One common type of secured debt occurs when a major asset such as a car, major appliances or a business is paid for over a period of time. Usually, the lender of credit will retain some measure of legal ownership in the asset—termed a security interest—until it is paid off. The law calls this type of debt a "purchase money secured debt" because it is incurred to purchase the property that serves as security for repayment.

Another common type of secured debt occurs when a lender, as a condition of the loan, takes a security interest in property already owned by the person applying for the money. For instance, most finance companies require their borrowers to agree to pledge "all their personal property" as security for the loan. The legal jargon for this type of security interest is a "non-purchase money secured debt"—that is, the debt is incurred for a purpose other than purchasing the property that secures repayment.

Other common types of secured debts are mortgages and deeds of trust owed on real estate in exchange for a purchase or equity loan, tax liens and assessments that are owed on real estate, and in some instances, liens (legal claims) on personal and real property created as a result of litigation or home repair activity.

If you are leaving property in your will that is subject to a secured debt, you will naturally be concerned about whether the debt will pass to the beneficiary along with the property, or whether it must be paid by your estate.

How WillMaker Handles Secured Debts

- **Debts owed on real estate** WillMaker passes all secured debts owed on real estate along with the real estate.

Example

Paul owes $50,000 under a deed of trust on his home, signed as condition of obtaining an equity loan. He leaves the home to his children. The deed of trust is a non-purchase money secured debt on real property and passes to the children along with the property.

Example

Steve and Catherine, a married couple, borrow $100,000 from the bank to purchase their home, and take out a deed of trust in the bank's favor as security for the loan. They still owe $78,000. In separate wills, Steve and Catherine leave their ownership share to each other and name their children as alternates to take the home in equal shares. The deed of trust is a purchase money secured debt and, if the children get the property, they will also get the mortgage.

Example

All is as set out in the example above, but Steve and Catherine are two years behind on their property taxes. The property taxes would pass to the children along with the home and the deed of trust obligation.

- **Debts owed on personal property** All purchase money secured debts owed on personal property pass to the beneficiaries of the personal property. However, non-purchase money secured debts owed on personal property do not pass with the property and are payable by your estate.

Example

Phil drives a 1985 Ferrari. Although the car is registered in Phil's name, the bank holds legal title pending Phil's payment of the outstanding $75,000 car note. Phil uses WillMaker to leave the car to his long-time companion Paula. The car note is a purchase money secured debt and will pass to Paula with the car.

Example

Carla borrowed $10,000 from a finance company to pay her income taxes. To get the money, she signed an agreement pledging "all her property" as collateral for repayment. Carla has a daughter, Juliet, and a son, Mark. Carla uses WillMaker to leave Juliet a precious doll house collection that has been passed down through the family for five generations, and leaves Mark the rest of her property. When Carla dies, she still owes $9,000 on the loan. The $9,000 debt is a non-purchase money secured debt and is payable out of Carla's estate. Carla can either provide how this—and any other debts— should be paid, or she can leave this decision up to her personal representative.

> ▶ **What If a Beneficiary Cannot Pay Off a Debt that**
> ▶ **Comes with the Property?**
> ▶ Because the property is usually worth more than any debt secured by it, an
> ▶ inheritor who does not want to owe money can sell the property, pay off the debt
> ▶ and pocket the difference. However, at times, relying on this approach is not
> ▶ satisfactory—especially when it comes to houses. For example, if you leave your
> ▶ daughter your house with the hope that it will be her home, you will probably not
> ▶ want her to have to sell the house because she cannot meet the mortgage
> ▶ payments. If you think a particular beneficiary will need assistance with paying a
> ▶ debt owed on property, try to leave the beneficiary the necessary money or
> ▶ valuable assets as either a specific or residuary bequest.

2. Unsecured Debts

Unsecured debts are all debts not tied to specific property. Common examples
are medical bills, most credit card bills, student loans, utility bills and probate
fees. Under WillMaker, these debts and expenses must be paid by your
personal representative (executor), either according to instructions in your
will, or as required by the laws of your state if you provide no instructions.

3. Canceling Debts Others Owe You

You can choose to release anyone who owes you a debt from the
responsibility of paying it back to your estate after you die. You can cancel
any such debt—oral or written. If you do, your forgiveness functions much the
same as giving a gift; those who were indebted to you will no longer be
legally required to pay the money they owed.

Of course, keep in mind that the gift you are giving to the person or
institution owing the debt will diminish the property that your beneficiaries
may receive under your will.

> **⚠** If you are married and forgiving a debt, first make sure you have the full power to do so. For example, if the debt was incurred while you were married, you may only have the right to forgive half the debt. There is a special need to be cautious about this possibility in community property states. If your debt is a community property debt, you cannot cancel the whole amount due unless your spouse agrees to allow you to cancel his or her share of the debt—and puts that agreement in writing.

C. Arranging For Payment of Debts and Probate Expenses

WillMaker offers three basic options for paying unsecured debts, including the expenses of probate. You can:

- leave no instructions, which will mean that your personal representative will pay the debts and expenses as required by the laws of your state;
- specify a particular asset or assets to be used or sold to pay debts and expenses; or
- specify that debts and expenses be paid out of your residuary estate.

1. Leave No Instructions to Pay Debts

If you do not specify in your will how you want your debts and expenses to be paid, your personal representative will be instructed by your will to follow your state's laws.

Some states require that debts and expenses be paid first out of property in your estate that does not pass under your will for some reason—for example, your residuary beneficiary and alternate both fail to survive you—and next from the residuary of your estate. In other states, your debts and expenses must first be paid out of liquid assets such as bank accounts and securities, then from tangible personal property, and as a last resort, from real estate.

If you decide not to use either of the debt payment options offered by WillMaker, your personal representative will be instructed by your will to follow your state's rules. Typically, you don't need to leave instructions about debts if:

- your debts and expenses are likely to be negligible—or represent a tiny fraction of a relatively large estate. You don't need to plan how debts resulting from normal monthly bills should be paid;

- you are leaving all your property to your spouse or specify that it should be shared among a very few beneficiaries, without divvying it up in specific bequests. In this situation, your debts will be paid first and then the beneficiaries will receive what's left; or

- you know and approve of the way your state deals with debts and expenses.

But you need to plan more carefully if debts payable by your estate are likely to be large enough to cut significantly into bequests left to individuals and charitable institutions. The danger, of course, is that unless you plan carefully, the people whose bequests are used to pay debts and expenses may be the very people who you would have preferred to fully inherit.

Example

Ruth has $40,000 in a money market account and several valuable musical instruments, also worth $40,000. She makes a will leaving the money market account to her daughter and the instruments to her musician son, but doesn't specify how her debts and expenses should be paid. Due to medical bills and an unpaid personal loan from a friend, Ruth dies owing $35,000. After Ruth's death, her personal representative must follow state law which first requires that debts be paid out of the residuary estate. But because there is no residuary—all property is used up by specific bequests—a second rule applies that requires that debts be paid out of liquid assets. As a result, the personal representative pays the $35,000 out of the money market account, leaving the daughter with only $5,000. The son receives the $40,000 worth of musical instruments.

Covering Your Debts with Insurance

One way to deal with the problem of large debts and small assets is to purchase a life insurance policy in an amount large enough to pay your anticipated debts and expenses, and have the proceeds made payable to your estate. You can then specify in your will that these proceeds should be used to pay your debts and expenses—with the rest going to your residuary beneficiary or a beneficiary named in a specific bequest.

But be forewarned. If large sums are involved, talk with an estate planner or accountant before adopting this sort of plan. Having insurance money paid to your estate subjects that amount to probate. A better alternative is often to provide that estate assets be sold, with the proceeds used to pay the debts. Then have the insurance proceeds made payable directly to your loved ones, free of probate.

2. Designate Specific Assets to Pay Debts

One good approach to taking care of unsecured debts and expenses your estate owes is to designate one or more specific assets that your personal representative must use to pay them. If you designate a savings or money market account, for example, to be used for paying off your debts and expenses, and the amount in the account is sufficient to meet these obligations, the other bequests you make in your will won't be affected by your estate's indebtedness.

Of course, if the source you specify is insufficient to pay all the bills, your personal representative will still face the problem of which property to use to make up the difference. For this reason, it's often wise to list several resources and specify the order in which they should be used. Also, make sure that they are worth more than what is likely to be required.

Example

Ella, a widow, makes a will that contains the following bequests:

- My house at 1111 Soto Street in Albany, New York to Hillary Bernette (The house has an outstanding mortgage of $50,000, for which Hillary will become responsible.)
- My coin collection (appraised at $30,000) to my three children, Stanley, Mark and Belinda;
- My three antique chandeliers to my brother Herbert;

- The rest of my property to my companion Denise. Although not spelled out in the will, this property consists of a savings account[1] ($26,000), a car ($5,000), a camera ($1,000) and stock ($7,000).

Using WillMaker, Ella specifies that her savings account and stock be used in the order listed to pay debts and expenses. When Ella dies, she owes $8,000; the expenses of probating her estate total $4,000. Following Ella's instructions, her personal representative would close the savings account, use $12,000 of it to pay debts and expenses, and turn the rest over to Denise along with the stock and camera.

Example

Now suppose Ella has only $6,000 in the savings account. When she dies, her personal representative, following the same instructions, would close the bank account ($6,000) and sell enough stock to make up the difference ($6,000). The remaining $1,000 worth of stock, the camera and the car would pass to Denise.

Selecting Specific Assets to Pay Debts

If you select specific assets to pay your debts and expenses, here are some tips on what assets to choose.

- **Select liquid assets over non-liquid assets** Liquid assets are those easily converted into cash at full value—bank and deposit accounts, money market accounts, stocks and bonds. On the other hand, tangible assets such as motor vehicles, planes, jewelry, stamp and coin collections, electronic items and musical instruments must be sold to raise the necessary cash. Hurried sales seldom bring in anywhere near the full value, which means the net worth of your estate will also be reduced.

---

[1]Ella could have planned to avoid probate by placing a lot of her property in a living trust. Certainly, instead of leaving the savings account as part of her residuary estate, Ella could have created a pay-on-death account (informal bank account trust) naming Denise as beneficiary. See Chapter 13 for an overview of various probate avoidance devices.

Example

Harry writes mystery books for a living. He has never produced a blockbuster but owns fifteen copyrights, which produce royalties of about $70,000 a year. During his life, Harry has traveled widely and collected artifacts from around the world. They have a value of $300,000 if sold carefully to knowledgeable collectors. Harry makes a will leaving his copyrights to his spouse and the artifacts to his children. He also designates that the artifacts should be used to pay his debts and expenses—which total $150,000 at death. Harry's personal representative, who is not a collector and has little time or inclination to sell the artifacts one by one, sells them in bulk for $140,000—less than half of their true value. To raise the extra $10,000, two of the copyrights are sold, again at less than their true value. As a result, Harry's children receive nothing and his spouse gets less than Harry intended. It would have been far better for Harry to purchase insurance to pay his debts or to sell some of his artifacts before his death for full value and pay off the debt.

- **Avoid designating property you have left to specific beneficiaries** As you know, WillMaker allows you to make up to 28 separate specific bequests as well as name a residuary beneficiary to take the rest of your property. It is important to review your specific bequests before designating assets to pay debts and expenses. If possible, designate liquid assets that have not been left to specific beneficiaries. Only as a last resort should you earmark a tangible item also left in a specific bequest for first use to pay debts and expenses.

  One exception to this general recommendation occurs if you believe you are unlikely to owe much when you die, and that the expenses of probate will be low. Then, it makes sense for you to designate a substantial liquid asset left as a specific bequest to also pay debts and expenses.

 ### Describe Property Consistently

Property designated both as a specific bequest and as a source for paying your debts should be described exactly the same in both instances to avoid confusion.

3. Designate Your Residuary Estate to Pay Debts

Using this WillMaker option, you direct your personal representative to pay all your debts and expenses out of your residuary estate—leaving it up to him or her which assets to use, and in which order. This option makes sense if you are leaving the bulk of your estate through specific bequests, and are using your residuary as a catch-all for property that comes into your estate after you make your will but before you die. But be sure there will be enough assets in your residuary to pay likely debts.

If your residuary bequest is an important part of your will—you make lots of bequests of specific property items and leave the bulk of your estate to your spouse through the residuary clause—then designating your residuary to pay debts may make less sense, especially if they are large enough to eat into the residuary. Instead, you may prefer to use the "specific asset" option discussed in Section 1, above. That would permit you to designate a specific asset for paying your debts and expenses and allow your spouse to receive the full amount in your residuary estate.

Designating your residuary to pay debts also makes sense if your residuary beneficiary is the same as one or more of the beneficiaries to whom you have already left specific bequests. For example, this would be the case if you leave the bulk of your estate to your spouse or children in a specific bequest and also name them as your residuary beneficiaries.

D. Paying Estate and Inheritance Taxes

Before you concentrate on how you want your estate and inheritance taxes to be paid, consider whether you need to be concerned about these types of taxes at all. Most people do not.

▶ Arranging to Pay Other Taxes

This discussion does not include back income or real property taxes owed by your estate. Real property taxes are secured debts, and pass to the beneficiary along with the real property. Income taxes must be paid out of your estate as discussed above.

Basically, if the net worth of your estate is less than $600,000 when you die—or you are leaving property of greater value all to your spouse—there will likely be no federal estate tax unless you made substantial gifts during your life.[2] And while some states impose separate taxes on estates of lesser

---

[2]As is explained in more detail in Chapter 13, Section D, if you give property worth more than $10,000 to an individual other than your spouse during a year, the excess is subtracted from your $600,000 exempt amount.

value, the taxes normally do not take a deep enough bite to cause serious concern unless your estate is very large.[3]

If the value of your estate is well below the federal and state tax range, and you have no reasonable expectation that your estate will grow to that level between the time you make your will and the time you die, skip the following discussion of your options for paying taxes. And, when asked by the program whether you wish to plan for the payment of taxes, answer no.

 ### Get Some Help for Large Estates

As you might imagine, financial planning experts have devised many creative ways to plan for paying estate and inheritance taxes. If your estate is large enough to warrant concern about possible federal estate and state inheritance taxes, it is large enough for you to afford a consultation with an accountant, estate planning specialist, or lawyer specializing in estates and trusts. Again, the threshold at which you need to worry about taxes is normally at least $600,000, and often much higher if you plan to leave much of your property to your spouse. (See Chapter 13 for an overview of estate planning techniques.)

If you are a relatively young, healthy person and your estate is only slightly larger than $600,000, you may want to adopt one of the WillMaker tax payment options now and worry about more sophisticated tax planning later. After all, by the time you die, federal and state tax rules will probably have been changed many times.

WillMaker offers the following options for paying your estate and inheritance taxes. You can:

1. leave no instructions;

2. designate specific assets;

---

[3]Many states impose no significant death taxes. Among those that do, the taxes are technically imposed on the beneficiaries of the estate rather than on the estate itself. However, your personal representative has an obligation to pay the taxes and will therefore deduct the taxes from each bequest unless you specify differently in your will, as you can do when using WillMaker. For a list of states that levy death taxes, see Chapter 13, Section E.

3. specify that the tax burden should be shared equitably among beneficiaries; or

4. specify that your tax liability be paid out of the residuary estate.

1. Leave No Instructions to Pay Taxes

If you choose not to leave instructions on how estate and inheritance taxes should be paid, WillMaker directs your personal representative to pay them as required by the laws of your state. As with your debts and expenses, your state law controls how your personal representative is to approach this issue if you do not establish your own plan. Some states leave the method of payment up to your personal representative, while others provide that all beneficiaries must share equitably in the tax burden. Depending on your financial and tax situation and the law of your state, more variables set in than can reasonably be covered here.

2. Designate Specific Assets to Pay Taxes

As with payment of debts and expenses, it may be a good approach to designate one or more specific property items to satisfy paying your taxes. Again, if you designate a bank, brokerage or money market account to be used for paying taxes, and the amount in the account is adequate to meet these obligations, the other bequests you make in your will should not be affected.

Of course, if the resource you specify for payment of your estate and inheritance taxes is insufficient to pay the amount due, your personal representative will still face the problem of which property will be used to make up the difference. So, again, it is a good idea to list several resources which should be used for payment of estate and inheritance taxes in the order listed.

Guidance for Selecting Specific Assets

If you do choose to select specific assets to be used to pay your taxes, follow the general rules set out in Section C, above.

---

3. Specify that Tax Payments Be Shared Equitably

For the purpose of computing estate and inheritance tax liability, your estate consists of all property you legally own at your death, whether it passes under the terms of your will or outside of your will—under a joint tenancy, living trust, savings bank trust or life insurance policy. Because your estate's tax liability will be computed on the basis of all this property, you may wish to have the beneficiaries of this property share proportionately in the responsibility for paying the taxes.

Example

Julie Johanssen, a widow, owns a house (worth $500,000), stocks ($200,000), jewelry ($150,000) and investments as a limited partner in a number of rental properties ($300,000). To avoid probate, Julie puts the house in a living trust for her eldest son Warren, the stocks in a living trust for another son Alain, and uses her will to leave the jewelry to a daughter Penelope and the investments to her two surviving brothers, Sean and Ivan. She specifies that all beneficiaries of property in her taxable estate share in paying any estate and inheritance taxes.

When Julie dies, the net worth of her estate, which consists of all the property mentioned, is $1,150,000. Because this taxable estate is over $600,000, there is federal estate tax liability.

Each of Julie's beneficiaries will be responsible for paying a portion of this liability. Each portion will be measured by the proportion that beneficiary's inheritance has to the estate as a whole. Under this approach, Warren will be responsible for approximately 43% of the tax, Penelope for 13%, and so on. For Warren, this would mean a tax liability of $175,139. Penelope would owe $52,949.

While this option may be the most equitable way to have your taxes paid, it may not be the best approach in some circumstances. For instance, if Warren is ill and cannot raise the money without selling the house, Julie may want to provide that at least his portion of the taxes should be paid from another designated source.

4. Designate Your Residuary Estate to Pay Taxes

In this option, you direct your personal representative to pay your estate and inheritance taxes out of your residuary estate—leaving it up to him or her to decide which assets are to be used, and in which order. This can be a wise choice if the money and property in the residuary is specifically placed there for this purpose.

Sometimes, however, it can be a mistake. It is particularly unwise when:

- your taxable estate is fairly large, with a number of assets being passed outside of probate; and

- you intend the residuary to be used for other purposes—such as to leave property to your children or to pass large sums to your spouse.

The problem, of course, is that if many valuable assets such as a house are passed outside the will—in a living trust, for example—there will be a hefty estate tax liability but little property in the residuary estate. If all taxes are to be paid by the residuary estate, there may be no money left for the residuary beneficiaries. You will likely want to plan so that taxes will not wipe out the residuary beneficiary's share while recipients of other property get off tax-free.

10 Making It Legal: Final Steps

Once you have proceeded through all the WillMaker screens and responded to all the questions posed, your will is complete. There are just a few more steps you must take to make your WillMaker will legally effective so that its instructions will be correctly implemented after your death.

A. Before You Sign

Before you sign your will, take some time to scrutinize it and make sure it accurately expresses your wishes.

1. Review Your Will

You can do this either by calling it up on the screen or by printing out a draft copy. Or if you believe in both a belt and suspenders, read both the screen and printed versions.

To see the will on the screen or print out a draft, follow the directions on the screen titled "Document Choices." (Consult the Users' Guide, Sections G and H, if you need additional guidance.) If, after you review the wording of your will, you want to make changes, use the review/modify option, also on the Document Choices screen.

2. Have Your Will Checked by an Expert

You may want to have your will checked by an attorney or tax expert. This makes good sense if you are left with nagging questions about the law or implications of your choices, or if you own a great deal of property or have a complicated idea of how you want to leave it. But keep in mind that you are your own best expert on what property you own, your relation to family members and friends and your own favorite charities—in short, most issues and decisions involved in making a will. Also, few attorneys support the self-help approach to making a will; you may be hard-pressed to find one who is cooperative. (See Chapter 14 for information on how to find and use a lawyer.)

B. Sign Your Will and Have It Witnessed

To be valid, a will must be legally "executed." This is not as bloody as it sounds. It means only that you must sign your will in front of witnesses. These witnesses must not only sign the will in your presence, but also in the presence of the other witnesses.

While state laws vary as to how many witnesses are required, three meets the minimum requirement of every state. Even if your state requires only two, it is better to have three people act as witnesses for your will. That will provide one more person to establish that your signature is valid if it is later contested in court, although that rarely happens.

1. Requirements for Witnesses

There are a few legal requirements for witnesses. They need only be:

- adults (in most states, 18 or older);
- of sound mind; and
- people who will not inherit under the will. Anyone to whom you leave property under your will, even as an alternate or residuary beneficiary, should not be a witness.

As a matter of common sense, the people you choose to be witnesses should be easily available when you die. While this bit of future history is impossible to foretell with certainty, it is best to choose witnesses who are in good health, younger than you are and who seem likely to remain in your geographic area. However, the witnesses do not have to be residents of your state.

2. Self-Proving Wills: A Probate Shortcut

For a will to be accepted by a probate court, the executor must show that the will really is the will of the person it purports to be—a process called "proving" the will. In the past, all wills were proved either by having one or two witnesses come into court to testify or swear in written, notarized statements called affidavits that they saw you sign your will.

▶
▶ **States without Standard Self-Proving Laws**
▶ The self-proving option is not available in the District of Columbia, Maryland,
▶ Michigan, Ohio and Vermont. In these states, your personal representative will be
▶ required to prove your will.
▶ And to comply with New Hampshire law, WillMaker handles the self-proving
▶ option a little differently for its residents. They are asked on a separate screen
▶ whether they wish to make their will self-proving. If so, the program prints out an
▶ affidavit as part of the will. The will should be witnessed and signed in front of a
▶ Notary Public.
▶ In California, the self-proving feature does not require a separate affidavit.
▶ Instead, the fact that the witnesses sign the will under oath is sufficient to have the
▶ will admitted into probate, unless a challenge is mounted.

Today, most states allow people to make their wills self-proving—that is, they can be admitted in probate court without the hassle of herding up witnesses to appear in court or sign affidavits. This is accomplished when the person making the will and the witnesses all appear before a Notary Public and sign a statement about the will's authenticity under oath.

When you print your will, WillMaker automatically produces a self-proving affidavit that is suitable for your state, with accompanying instructions. The self-proving affidavit is not part of your will, but a separate document. To use it, you and your witnesses must first sign the will as discussed above. Then, you and your witnesses must sign the self-proving affidavit in front of a Notary Public. This may be done any time after the will is signed, but obviously, it is easiest to do it while all your witnesses are gathered together to watch you sign your will.

Many younger people—who are likely to make a number of subsequent wills before they die—decide not to make their wills self-proving, due to the initial trouble of getting a Notary to attend the signing. If you are one of these people, file the uncompleted affidavit and instructions in a safe place in case you change your mind later.

3. Signing Procedure

You need not utter any magic words when signing your will and having it witnessed, but a few legal requirements suggest the best way to proceed:

- Gather all three witnesses together in one place.

- Inform your witnesses that the papers you hold in your hand are your last will and testament. This is important, because the laws in many states specifically require that you acknowledge the document as your will before the witnesses sign it. The witnesses need not read your will, however, and there is no need for them to know its contents.

- Initial each page of the will at the bottom on the lines next to the "initial" line. The purpose of initialing is to prevent anyone from challenging the will as invalid because changes were made to it by someone else.

- Sign the last page on the signature line *in the witnesses' presence*. When you sign the will, use the same form of your name as you provided when WillMaker asked you to input your name on the screen. Again, this should be the form of the name you most commonly use to sign legal documents such as deeds, checks and loan applications.

- Ask the witnesses to initial the bottom of each page on the same "initial" line you did, then watch as they sign and fill in their addresses on the last page where indicated. Their initials act as evidence if anyone later claims you changed your will without going through the proper legal formalities. If you don't want your witnesses to see what is in your will when they are initialing the pages, cover each page.

(See also Section 2, above, "Self-Proving Wills: A Probate Shortcut.")

▶ **Make Sure Witnesses Sign on a Page with Text**

If the final page of your will contains only spaces for the signatures of your witnesses, and no text of your will, it is remotely possible that after your death someone might claim that the witness page was illegally added later and that the will itself was not properly signed and witnessed.

To avoid this, change the number of lines per page by a line or two on the print set-up screen to alter the way the will prints out, so that either:

- some text of the will appears on the last page before the witness lines, or
- at least one of the witness lines appears on the next-to-last page.

C. Do Not Make Changes To Your Will

Once you have produced and printed a will using WillMaker, it is extremely important that you not alter it by inserting handwritten or typed additions or changes—either before or after you sign it. Do not even correct misspellings. The laws of most states require that after a will is signed, any additions or changes to it, even clerical ones, must be made by following the same signing and witnessing requirements as for an original will. Although it is legally possible to make handwritten corrections before you sign, it is a bad idea, since after your death, it will not be clear to the probate court that you made

the corrections before the will was signed. The possibility that the changes
were made later may throw the legality of the whole will into question.

> **Note for Perfectionists: No Accents or Umlauts**
>
> WillMaker does not allow you to use special characters, such as an accent mark or
> an umlaut. You may be tempted to ink one in where your name, or the name of a
> beneficiary, carries the mark in question. Don't. The fact that the character is
> missing may be displeasing to you, but it will have no adverse impact on your
> will's legality or effectiveness. Minor spelling errors, typos and even the awkward
> wording of text that you enter also will not adversely affect the legality of your
> will.

D. WillMaker Does Not Allow Codicils

If you want to make changes once your will has been signed and witnessed,
the law allows you two ways to accomplish it: You can either make a new
will, or make a formal addition, called a codicil, to the existing one.

One of the great advantages of WillMaker is that you can conveniently
keep up-to-date by simply putting the WillMaker disk into your computer and
making a new will. This does away with the need to tack in changes to the
will in the form of a codicil. Codicils are not allowed when using WillMaker
because of the possibility of creating a conflict between the codicil and the
original will.

E. Storing Your Will

Once your will is properly signed and witnessed, your main consideration is
that your personal representative can easily locate it at your death. Here are
some suggestions:

• Store your printed and witnessed will in an envelope on which you have
  typed your name and the word "Will"—or use the preprinted envelope that
  comes with the WillMaker program.

- Place the envelope in a fireproof metal box, file cabinet or home safe. An alternative is to place the original copy of your will in a safe deposit box. But before doing that, learn the bank's policy about access to the box after your death. If, for instance, the safe deposit box is in your name alone, the box can probably be opened only by a person authorized by the court and, then, only in the presence of a bank employee. An inventory may even be required if any person enters the box or for state tax purposes. All of this takes time, and in the meantime, your will is locked away from those who need access to it.

▶ Helping Others Find Your Will

Your will should be easy to locate at your death. You don't want your loved ones to undergo the anxiety of having to search for your will when they are already dealing with the grief of losing you. Make sure your personal representative, and at least one other person you trust, know where to find your will.

And while you're at it, making a clear record of all your property, its location and the location of any ownership documents that relate to it will make your executor's job easier. *For the Record*, a software program by Carol Pladsen & Ralph Warner (Nolo Press) offers an excellent way to do this.

F. Making Copies of Your Will

Some people are tempted to prepare more than one signed and witnessed original of their will in case one is lost. While it is legal in most states to prepare and execute duplicate originals, it is not a good idea. Common sense tells you why: If you later want to change your will, it can be difficult to locate all the old ones to destroy them.

It can sometimes be a good idea, however, to make several unsigned copies of your current will. Give one to your proposed personal representative (executor). And, if it is appropriate, give other copies to your spouse, friends or children. In a close family, it can be a relief to everyone to learn your plans for distributing your property. But obviously, there are all sorts of good reasons why you may wish to keep the contents of your will strictly confidential until your death. If so, you should not make any copies.

G. Give the WillMaker Disk a Good Home

Once you have printed out your will, you still have a copy of it in electronic form—on your disk. It is best to find a safe, private place to store the disk so that you can use it to update your will if that becomes necessary. Others should not have access to the disk without your permission.

If you have used your hard disk to run WillMaker, it is a good idea to copy the files to a floppy disk. Then, label and store the floppy disk and delete the WillMaker files from your hard disk. This will lessen the chance that your will files will be altered.

▶ **Note**
▶ As with other unsigned and unwitnessed copies, the copy of your will stored on
▶ the WillMaker disk does not constitute a valid will until it is printed out and
▶ formally signed and witnessed as discussed above.

11 Keeping Your Will Up-to-Date

This chapter alerts you to life changes that require you to make a new will.

Your will is an extremely personal document. Your marital status, where you live, what kind and how much property you own and whether you have children are all examples of life choices that affect what you include in your will and what laws will be applied to enforce it.

But your life changes. You may sell one house and buy another. You may divorce. You may have or adopt children. Eventually you will face the grief associated with the death of a loved one. Not all life changes require that you also change your will. However, significant ones often do.

A. When You Should Make a New Will

You should make a new will:

1. If your marital status changes

Suppose that after you use WillMaker to leave all or part of your property to your spouse, you get divorced. Under the law in many states, the divorce automatically cancels the bequest to the ex-spouse. The alternate beneficiary named for that bequest, or, if there is none, your residuary beneficiary, gets the property. In some states, however, your ex-spouse would still inherit as directed in the will. If you remarry, state legal rules become even more murky.

Rather than deal with all these complexities, follow this simple rule: Make a new will if you marry, divorce or if you are separated and seriously considering divorce.

 If you indicate a change in marital status, WillMaker does not return you directly to the review menu. Instead, it takes you back through your previous answers and asks you to verify them. The reason for this is that many willmaking decisions are based on marital status. If your marital status changes, you should carefully review whether your property is going to the people you want to get it—and whether your spouse is receiving an adequate share.

 If you leave your spouse out of your will because you are separated, and you die before you become divorced, it is possible that the spouse could claim a statutory share of your estate. (Statutory shares are explained in Chapter 4, Section C.) Consult a lawyer to find out how the laws of your state apply to this situation.

2. If the property you own changes significantly and you made specific bequests

If you leave all property through your residuary clause, there is no need to change your will if you acquire new items of property or get rid of existing ones—your residuary beneficiary takes all of your property at your death.

If you leave a specific item to someone, however—a particular Tiffany lamp, for example—but you no longer own the item when you die, the person named in the will to receive it is out of luck. He or she obviously cannot have the actual item, and is not entitled to receive another item or money in lieu of it.[1] Lawyers call such a failure of a bequest "ademption." People who don't inherit the property in question are often heard to use an earthier term.

A similar problem occurs when there is not enough money to go around. For example, if you leave $50,000 each to your wife and two children, but there is only $100,000 in your estate at your death, the gifts in the will must be reduced. In legal lingo, this is called an "abatement." How property is abated under state law is often problematic; adjust the amount of your bequests to the size of your estate to avoid this.

3. If you adopt or have additional children

Each time a child is born or legally adopted into your family, the new child should be named in the will—where you are asked to name your children— and provided for according to your wishes. If you fail to do this, the child might later challenge your will in court, claiming that he or she was overlooked as an heir and is entitled to a substantial share of your property. (See Chapter 7, Section A.)

---

[1] In some circumstances, if a specific item has merely changed form, the original beneficiary may still have a claim to it. Examples of this are:
- a promissory note has been paid and the cash is still available; and
- a house which has been sold in exchange for a promissory note and deed of trust.

> ⚠ If you indicate that you now have a minor child, WillMaker does not return you directly to the review menu. Instead, it takes you back through your previous answers and asks you to verify them. It also will ask you to name a personal guardian and alternate personal guardian to care for the child if he or she is a minor when you die and the child's other parent is dead or unavailable.

4. If your child dies, leaving children

If any of your children die before you, and leave children (your grandchildren), those grandchildren should also be named in your will—where you are asked to name the children of a deceased child. If they are not mentioned in your will, they might later be legally entitled to claim a share of your estate.

5. If you move to a different state

WillMaker applies several state-specific laws when it helps you create your will. These laws are especially important in two situations:

- If you have set up one form of management for young beneficiaries and then move to a different state, you may find when making a new will that WillMaker presents you with different management options. This is because some states have adopted the Transfers to Minors Act and others have not. If you want to see whether your new state offers different management options, consult Chapter 7, Section E.

- If you are married and are not leaving all or most of your property to your spouse, review the property ownership information in Chapter 4 if you move from a community property state to a common law state or vice-versa.

When you change your state, WillMaker does not return you directly to the review menu. Instead, it takes you back through your previous answers and asks you to verify them. It also erases any provisions you have made to provide management for property left to minors or young adults, and asks you to reconsider this issue. The reason for this is that different states provide different options for property management.

6. If any of your beneficiaries die

If a beneficiary you have named to receive a significant amount of property either as a specific or residuary beneficiary dies before you, you should make a new will. It is especially important to do this if you named only one beneficiary for the bequest and failed to name an alternate—or if the alternate you named is no longer your first choice to get the property.

7. If the person you named as personal guardian for your minor children or manager for their property is no longer available to serve

The first choice or alternate named to serve as a personal guardian for your minor children or manager for their property may move away, become disabled, or simply turn out to be someone you consider unsuitable for the job. If so, you will probably want to make a new will naming somebody else.

8. If the person or institution named as personal representative (executor) is no longer able to serve

The personal representative or executor of your estate is responsible for making sure your will provisions are carried out. If you decide that the personal representative you named originally is no longer suitable, you may want to name another.

9. If your witnesses move away, die or are no longer competent

The witnesses who sign your will are responsible for testifying that your will or your signature on it is valid. If two or more of your witnesses become unable to fulfill this function, you may want to make a new will with new witnesses—especially if you have some inkling that anyone is likely to contest your will after you die. But a new will is probably not necessary if you have made your will self-proving. (See Chapter 10, Section B.)

B. How To Make a New Will

If you want to make a new will, a subsequent swoop through the WillMaker program will proceed even more quickly than the first time through, since you will know what to expect and will likely be familiar with many of the legal concepts you had to learn the first time through.

Here is how to make a new will:

- Start up the WillMaker program. Unless you have run the program since printing your will, the program should produce the final program screen.

- Choose the section of your will that you wish to change. Repeat this to make any other changes you wish. Once you are finished making all the changes, click OK.

- Go to the File menu and select Preview Will to review the text of your new will to make sure you are satisfied that your responses are accurate and the will reflects your wishes. You can do this by first looking at the entire will on the screen. You can doublecheck your will by printing out a copy. Or, if you wish, you can opt to store your will for a while before reviewing and printing it. Sometimes, looking at a document with fresh eyes gives you a fresh perspective.

- When you are satisfied with your new will, print it out—or create a text file and print the will from your word processor. (See the Users' Guide, Section H.)

- Following the directions in Chapter 10, Section B, sign your new will in the presence of witnesses and have them initial each page.

If you make a new will, even if it only involves a few changes, you must follow the legal requirements for having it signed and witnessed just as if you were starting from scratch. If you choose to make your will self-proving, you must also complete a new affidavit.

C. Making Your New Will Valid

As soon as you print, sign and have your new will witnessed, it will automatically replace all wills you have made before it. But to avoid possible confusion, you should physically destroy all other original wills and any copies of them.

12 Letters and Last Wishes

A. Expressing Sentiments or Explaining Choices

In addition to the tasks that you can accomplish by using WillMaker, you may also wish to:

- explain why gifts are being given to certain beneficiaries and not to others;

- explain disparities in gifts;

- express positive or negative sentiments about a beneficiary;

- explain why you are nominating a certain person as personal guardian for your minor children; or
- make sure your pet is cared for after your death.

WillMaker does not allow you to do these things in your will for one important reason: The program has been written, tested and re-tested with painstaking attention to allowing you to make your own legal and unambiguous will.

WillMaker does not allow you to enter general information, personal statements, or reasons for making or not making a bequest. That would risk the possibility that a person making the will might unwittingly produce a document with conflicting, confusing or possibly even illegal provisions.

Fortunately, there is a way you can have your final say about personal matters without risking your will's legal integrity. This is to write a letter to accompany your will expressing your thoughts to those who survive you.

Since what you put in the letter will not have legal effect as part of your will, there is no danger that your expressions will tread upon the time-tested legal language of the will or cause other problems later. Nevertheless, writing a letter to your loved ones to explain why you wrote your will as you did— and knowing they will read your reasoning at your death—can give you a great deal of peace of mind during life.

An Introduction for Your Letters

Here is a formal introduction that makes it clear that the letter you write to attach to your will is an expression of your sentiments and not intended as a will, codicil or interpretation of your will.

To My Personal Representative:

This letter expresses my feelings and reasons for certain decisions made in my will. It is not my will, nor do I intend it to be an interpretation of my will. My will, which was signed by me, dated and witnessed on _____ is the sole expression of my intentions concerning all my property, and other matters covered in it.

Should anything I say in this letter conflict with, or seem to conflict with, any provision of my will, the will provision shall be followed.

I request that my personal representative give a copy of this letter to each person named in my will to inherit property, or act as a guardian or custodian, and to anyone else my personal representative determines should receive a copy.

After this introduction, you are free to express your sentiments, keeping in mind that your estate may be held liable for any false, derogatory statements you make about an individual or organization. There is little useful that a book such as this can say to guide highly personal expressions of the heart. What follows are some suggestions about things you might wish to cover.

1. Explaining Why Gifts Were Made

The WillMaker requirement that you must keep descriptions of property and beneficiaries short and succinct may leave you dissatisfied. You have thought hard and long about why you want a particular person to get particular property—and are constrained in your will to listing your wishes in a few bloodless words. You can remedy that by explaining the whys and wherefores of your will directives.

Example

[Introduction]

The gift of my fishing boat to my friend Hank is in remembrance of the many companionable days we enjoyed fishing together on the lake. Hank, I hope you're out there for many more years.

or

Julie, the reason I have given you the farm is that you love it as much as I do and I know you'll do your best to make sure it stays in the family. But please, if the time comes when personal or family concerns mean that it makes sense to sell it, do so with a light heart—and knowing that it's just what I would have done.

2. Explaining Disparities in Gifts

You may also wish to explain your reasons for leaving more property to one person than another. While it is certainly your prerogative to make unequal bequests, you can also guess that in a number of family situations, they may cause hurt feelings or hostility after your death. Ideally, you could call those involved together during your life, explaining to them why you plan to leave your property as you do. However, if you wish to keep your property plans private until after you die—or would find such a lifetime meeting too painful or otherwise impossible—you can cure the uncomfortability by attaching a letter of explanation to your will.

Example

[Introduction]

I love all my children equally. The reason I gave a smaller percentage of my residuary estate to Tim than to my other children is that Tim received family funds to purchase a house, so it is fair that my other two children receive more of my property now.

or

I am giving the bulk of my property to my son John for one reason: because of his health problems, he needs it more.

Ted and Ellen, I love you just as much, and I am extremely proud of the life choices you have made. But the truth is that you two can manage fine without a boost from me, and John can't.

3. Expressing Positive or Negative Sentiments

Whatever your plans for leaving your property, you may wish to attach a letter to your will in which you clear your mind of some sentiments you formed during life. These may be positive—thanking a loved one for kind acts, or negative—explaining why you are leaving a person out of your will.

Example

[Introduction]

The reason I left $10,000 to my physician Dr. Buski is not only that she treated me competently over the years but that she was unfailingly gentle and attentive. I always appreciated that she made herself available—day or night—and took the time to explain my ailments and treatments to me.

or

I am leaving nothing to my brother Malcolm. I wish him no ill will. But over the years, he has decided to isolate himself from me and the rest of the family and I don't feel I owe him anything.

4. Explaining Your Choice for Personal Guardian

Having children is the biggest impetus for people to write their wills—and their prime concern is usually making sure that someone loving and competent will care for their children if the parents die while their children are still young. (See Chapter 7, Section C for a discussion of naming a personal guardian for minor children.) As noted, the person you name in your will as personal guardian does not automatically take over the job: a court must sanction the choice. However, your choice will likely be accepted unless the court deems that the best interests of the child would better be served in another arrangement—or you have bypassed the other parent who normally takes legal precedence.

If you do name someone as personal guardian who might not be the first logical choice—the other surviving parent or a close relative—it is a good idea to attach a letter to your will pointing up your reasons. This will give you an opportunity to explain to the court why naming the person you have selected as guardian is in the best interests of your children.

Example

[Introduction]

I have nominated my companion, Peter Nickol, to be the guardian of my daughter Melissa, because I know he would be the best guardian for her. For the past six years, Peter has functioned as Melissa's parent, living with me and her, helping to provide care for her, and loving her. She loves him and regards him as her father. She hardly knows her natural father, Tom Damm. She has not seen him for four years. He has not contributed to her support or taken any interest in her. If he were granted custody, Melissa would be taken from familiar surroundings and necessarily undergo emotional torment.

5. Providing Care for Your Pet

Legally, pets are property. Many pet owners, of course, disagree. They feel a true bond with their animals and want to make sure that when they die, their pets will get good care and a good home. The best way to do this is to make a formal arrangement. Unfortunately, you cannot leave money or other property to your pet, either through a will or trust. Instead, the best legal approach is to use your will to leave your pet—and perhaps some money for the expenses of its care and feeding—to someone you trust to look out for it.

Make the bequest of pet and money in a specific bequest screen in your WillMaker will. Then attach a letter to your will explaining your wishes to the new owner, and include special instructions for the pet's care. Of course, make sure you get the new owner's welcome approval before making such a bequest.

Example

[Introduction]

I have left my dog Spot to my neighbor Belinda Mason, because she has been a willing and loving friend to him—grooming him willingly and well and taking him for walks when I was on vacation or unwell. I know that Belinda and her three children will provide a loving and happy home for Spot when I no longer can.

I request that Belinda continue to take Spot for his tri-annual check-ups with the veterinarian in town, Dr. Schuler, and have left her $2,000 to help cover the cost of that care.

B. Funeral Requests

Many people have specific ideas for a ceremony to be held after their deaths—a meaningful church, synagogue or other place as the setting, a particular priest, pastor, rabbi or friend to officiate, a special song, poem or prayer to be included. Others prefer no pomp or circumstance, or perhaps a brief gathering of friends. Usually, a surviving spouse, child or close friend arranges these details. But if there is no one to do this for you—or if you simply want to provide others with guidance, it is a good idea to prepare a formal written letter setting out your wishes. Attach a copy to your will. But because it may take time and effort to locate your will after you die, you should make another copy, keep it in a safe and accessible place and make it known to whoever will have the responsibility to carry out the plans.

In addition, especially if your wishes are complicated or expensive, it is a good idea to arrange to pay for your funeral in advance, notifying survivors of what you have done.

Should you be unsure about alternatives for your own funeral, consider contacting one in a growing number of funeral societies—private, nonprofit organizations devoted to providing paying members with simple, dignified burials at a reasonable cost.

To locate a funeral society near you, check the telephone book, or contact:

The Continental Association of Funeral and Memorial Societies
7910 Woodmont Avenue; Suite 1208
Bethesda, MD 20814
301/913-0030

C. Disposal of Bodily Remains

You may also wish to specify in writing what should happen to your bodily remains. It may be difficult for you to think of such plans now. But sorrow, religious conviction, or community conventions may take hold of your surviving loved ones and cloud their decisions about how, when and where to arrange for disposing of your body. Some state laws require burial within a set number of days after death. And hospital or nursing home personnel are anxious to rid their institutions of dead bodies. There will be these and other pressures on your survivors to act quickly after your death.

In some families, people and financial resources are readily available to take care of all the details surrounding a death, and there is no reason for you to leave instructions. Often, though, you can help your survivors by recording your wishes. Under the laws in many states, written burial instructions of a deceased person are binding—as long as they do not violate any local legal restrictions on disposing of bodily remains. Even where there are no laws on the books making final requests binding, it is rare that a deceased person's written statement as to what should be done with his or her remains is not followed.

If you are on the outs with your close relatives, it is particularly important to leave instructions, because unless you leave a written directive, your next of kin have the legal right to make decisions about disposing of your body. For example, unmarried couples who live together often want to leave burial and funeral instructions with their partners to prevent disapproving family members from imposing their own plans. If you prepare such instructions, do so in a letter.

Here is a brief outline of some of the issues you might want to consider when it comes to providing for your body.

1. Donating Your Organs

If you want to leave your body to help in scientific study, you have two choices—both of which you must make clear to others during your lifetime:

- You can leave your entire body to medical science, usually a medical school; or
- You can donate certain body organs or tissues to transplant facilities.

You cannot usually do both. With the sole exception of an eye transplant, medical schools generally will not accept a body from which a part has been removed. If you wish to donate your body, contact a nearby medical school to see what legalities and forms are required.

Also, every state has adopted the Uniform Anatomical Gift Act, which ensures that every mentally competent adult can legally promise to make an after-death organ donation. A local doctor or hospital should be aware of what is required in your state.

For more information on donating any organ or tissue, contact:

The National Kidney Foundation
30 East 33rd Street
New York, NY 10016
212/889-2210
800/662-9010

2. Cremation

Cremation means burning a body. Legally, there are few constraints on
cremation—although most state laws now forbid crematoriums from requiring
that the needless expense of a casket be used during the cremation. Also, all
states and many localities have legal strictures against scattering cremated
ashes. Where it is allowed, a permit is usually required—whether the
scattering is to be over land or sea.

Whether your body is cremated or buried is your choice. If you wish to be
cremated, it is a good idea to make all arrangements in advance. And, as
discussed above, leave specific written instructions—again, attaching them to
your will and leaving another copy with a trusted friend or relative.

3. Burials

The law requires that all bodies must be disposed of in a sanitary way. Unless
there is a cremation with scattering ashes, this usually means the remains will
be buried or interred. There are normally two aspects to this, each traditionally
carried out by a separate business charged with preparing the body and
burying it.

Commercial funeral homes will generally take care of the paperwork
following a death, such as completing or obtaining death and burial
certificates. Most will also arrange to have the body removed from the place of
death, and will prepare it, usually by embalming. Contrary to common belief,
embalming is not usually required by law; it is only necessary if a body is
being transported by common carrier or in very rare instances, to curb the

spread of contagious disease. Many funeral homes will also arrange to have the body buried at a local cemetery, if that is your wish.

Most American cemeteries are privately-owned—and charge for burials including fees for the plot, grave liner, opening, closing and upkeep of the grave.

Many people also opt to provide for their own eventual burials by "pre-purchasing" a plot they pay for during life—often next to other family members. This removes the need to make separate burial directives that you attach to your will. Beware, however, of businesses that tack on exorbitant charges for things such as "perpetual care" of the plot and surrounding grounds. In reality, gravesites require very little upkeep. And you may well wish that the money were spent on things you could enjoy during your lifetime.

If you have specific ideas on how and where you want to be buried, express them in a letter—one copy of which should be attached to your will.

13 Estate Planning

Preparing a basic will such as the one produced by WillMaker is the essential first step in planning any estate. Especially for larger estates, however, many more options are available. This chapter provides a brief overview of what may be involved.

 Estate Planning Resources from Nolo Press

Nolo Press publishes several resources that can help you with estate planning. Understandably you may conclude that this makes our recommendation a little prejudiced, but we believe these are the best book and software products available, and offer a money-back guarantee if you do not agree.

- *Plan Your Estate.* Shows how to prepare an estate plan without the expensive services of a lawyer. It includes all the tear-out forms and step-by-step instructions to let people prepare living trusts and other estate planning devices. Goes into considerable detail on federal estate taxes and simple strategies to avoid them.

- *For the Record.* An easy-to-use software program that provides a single place to keep a complete inventory of all your important legal, financial, personal and family records. Having accurate and complete records gets you organized, makes tax preparation easier and helps loved ones manage your affairs if you become incapacitated or die. Information can be easily entered, changed and printed.

- *Elder Care: A Consumer's Guide to Choosing & Financing Long-Term Care.* A compendium of alternatives for those concerned about finding and financing long-term care. This book will help everyone involved—the older person in need of care, as well as the spouse, family and friends of the older person—deal with the difficult decisions in evaluating and paying for health care. It discusses planning so that an elder's financial resources can supplement money available from public sources.

- *A Legal Guide for Lesbian and Gay Couples.* A complete guide to understanding the specialized interpretations and laws that affect gay and lesbian couples, this book includes a chapter on estate planning concerns.

- *The Living Together Kit.* Much the same as *A Legal Guide for Lesbian and Gay Couples,* except the legal and estate planning planning advice is geared to the needs of unmarried heterosexual couples.

- *The Power of Attorney Book.* Step-by-step instructions for preparing a "durable power of attorney" that authorizes someone to make health care or financial decisions on your behalf if you become unable to do so.

See the back of this book for ordering information.

A. Do You Need More Than a Simple Will?

After using WillMaker to prepare a simple will, you may want to do additional estate planning to:

- avoid probate;

- reduce or limit death taxes; or

- control how property left to one or more beneficiaries, such as a surviving spouse or a child, can be used.

Not surprisingly, these estate planning objectives are of interest primarily to people who own substantial property. Tax planning, especially, is the province of larger estates, because there are no federal estate taxes on the first $600,000 passed to one's inheritors.[1] Planning to avoid probate or place controls on the future use of property can make sense for smaller estates, but people who have little to leave their inheritors will find there is little incentive to engage in sophisticated estate planning.

Even people with larger estates should face a blunt truth: Estate planning benefits your inheritors, not you. And your inheritors will not benefit from your time and trouble until you die, which may be many years from now. In the meantime, healthy people who expect to live for many more years often waste time, effort and money planning and replanning their estates every couple years to keep current.

---

[1]This assumes that the deceased person has not made substantial gifts of valuable property during life. See Section C below for more on federal estate and gift taxes.

Although you will rarely find a high-priced lawyer or financial planner who will admit it, it makes sense for many relatively healthy people with moderate-sized estates to rely primarily on a simple will and maybe several other fairly easy to use probate avoidance devices, but to postpone others until they reach late middle age or face a life-threatening illness.

Deciding whether or not to plan to avoid probate involves at least three considerations:

- **Your age** If you're under 60 or so and healthy, it probably makes sense to prepare a will, adopt the easier types of probate avoidance devices such as joint tenancy or pay-on-death bank accounts and leave the more complicated estate planning until later.

- **The size of your estate** The bigger your estate, the bigger the potential probate cost and tax liability. And the more reason to take steps to keep both at a minimum. Often with a large estate, it makes good sense to concentrate energy on seeing that major assets, such as real estate or business assets, are owned in a way that will avoid probate.

- **The type of property you own and how active you are in business** Some kinds of property are relatively easy to transfer directly to inheritors without a year's detour through probate—such as the bank balance in a pay-on-death account. Others are somewhat workier. For example, if you prepare a revocable living trust, you must keep it up-to-date, which can involve considerable time and trouble if you buy and sell a lot of property.

- **How much effort you're willing to expend** Planning to avoid probate typically saves your inheritors 5% to 7% of the value of your estate and allows them to get their inheritance more quickly. You must decide how much time, trouble and expense you are willing to undergo to achieve these benefits.

B. Planning to Avoid Probate

This section summarizes the principal ways to avoid probate. But first, here is a brief discussion of probate and why you may want to avoid it.

1. What is Probate?

Probate is the legal process that includes filing a deceased person's will with a court, locating and gathering his or her assets, paying debts and death taxes and eventually distributing what is left as the will directs. With the exceptions noted below, property left by will must, by law, go through probate. If there is no will and no probate avoidance devices were used, property is distributed according to state law—and it still must go through probate. Fortunately, property left using other legal devices, including joint tenancy and revocable living trusts, is not required to go through probate. It can be transferred directly to its inheritors.

► Small Estates May Be Exempt from Probate

Most states allow very small estates, usually in the $5,000 to $60,000 range, to pass to inheritors either free of probate or subject to a streamlined, do-it-yourself probate process. This is true even if you make a will and do not adopt any probate avoidance devices. Some states also simplify or eliminate the normal probate process for property left by one spouse to the other. *(Plan Your Estate: Wills, Probate Avoidance, Trusts & Taxes* by Denis Clifford (Nolo Press) contains a 50-state chart summarizing these laws.)

2. Why Avoid Probate

Probate has many drawbacks and few advantages. It typically takes from nine to 18 months, and is costly, involving fees for attorneys, appraisers, accountants and the probate court. All these costs are paid from estate property—reducing the amount left for inheritors. Fees which are set by state law or local custom vary somewhat, but often consume from 5% to 7% of an estate. Not surprisingly, the major cost is for lawyers. Either by custom or law, a probate lawyer's fees are typically a percentage of the estate's value, even if the work involves no more than transferring the property to a surviving spouse or dividing it among several children. Even worse, in a few states, the lawyer's fees are based on the value of the property that goes through probate, without subtracting what the deceased person owed on the property.

Example

If Harry, a resident of California, dies with a gross estate—that's the total value of everything he owns, without subtracting debts owed on the property—of $500,000, the standard attorney's fees under that state's probate fee statute would be $11,500. The fee is based on the $500,000 figure, even if Harry's house has a $200,000 mortgage on it. Harry's relatives would be free to try to negotiate a lower fee with the lawyer—but the lawyer is unlikely to mention that when quoting the statutory fee. Court filing fees, property appraisals and other costs would typically add thousands more. And if the probate involves anything beyond preparing routine paperwork, it may cost even more.

The fundamental problem with probate is that most consumers receive little value for their money. In most situations, an executor of the will, or close relative if there is no will, could pay debts and taxes and transfer property to inheritors quickly and safely without probate court supervision—for much less than the typical probate lawyer's fee. Unless relatives are fighting, or there are big claims against the estate, court intervention is usually unnecessary.

There is one advantage of probate. It sets a deadline by which creditors who have been properly notified of the probate proceeding must file formal claims against the estate. People worried about big claims—a person with a lot of debts or a professional who might face malpractice suits—sometimes want the cut-off date.

3. Ways to Avoid Probate

There are six major ways to transfer property so that it avoids probate at your death:

- Pay-on-death accounts
- Joint tenancy
- Revocable living trusts
- Retirement accounts
- Life insurance
- Gifts made during your life

Pay-on-Death Bank Accounts (Informal Trusts)

Banks and savings and loans allow you to name someone to receive, at your death, any money remaining in your account. No probate is required. Anyone with a checking, savings, or bank money market account or a certificate of deposit need only add a designation that the money be held in trust for a named beneficiary. Depending on local custom and state law, these accounts are called "pay-on-death," "savings bank" or "informal trust" accounts.

A particularly attractive feature of these pay-on-death accounts is that the person who establishes the account retains complete control over the money until his or her death. The beneficiary has no right to the money until the person who established the account dies. The depositor can withdraw all the money or change the beneficiary any time before death.

Because it is so easy to accomplish, it makes sense for almost everyone with a substantial amount of money in the bank to use this technique—no matter their age or the size of their estate.

▶ U.S. Government Securities

▶ Pay-on-death designations can also be used with United States Government Bonds, Treasury Bills and Treasury notes. As with bank accounts, the pay-on-death designation allows the securities to go directly to the beneficiary, without probate.

Gifts Made During Your Life

Another simple way to keep property out of probate is to give property away during your life—even shortly before death. Anything you give away while you are alive is not part of your estate when you die, so it is not subject to probate. To make a legal gift, you must surrender ownership and control over the property. It's not enough to claim to give property away if for the rest of your life you hold onto it and continue to control it as if no gift had been made.

Note   Section D1 of this chapter discusses the impact of gifts on federal estate and gift taxation.

Life Insurance

Americans have a tendency to over-insure their lives. Still, some life insurance can be useful, even essential, when a person must provide for children or disadvantaged dependents. The proceeds of a life insurance policy pass to its beneficiaries free of probate as long as a specific beneficiary is named. Normally, all that is needed to collect the proceeds is a certified copy of the death certificate. However, if you designate your own estate as the policy beneficiary, as is occasionally done when the estate will need immediate cash to pay debts or taxes, the proceeds will be subject to probate.

Retirement Accounts (IRAs, Keoghs and 401K Plans)

While retirement accounts were not designed as estate planning devices, they can be efficiently used that way. Funds in a person's retirement account at death pass to the beneficiary designated in the account documents and are not subject to probate. Although the retiree must withdraw a minimum amount—the sum varies each year, based on the person's life expectancy—beginning at age 70 1/2, the rest can stay in the account.

Community Property Note: In community property states (see Chapter 4, Section C for a list), one-half of the money put in a retirement account while a couple is married belongs to the surviving spouse.

Joint Tenancy with Right of Survivorship

Joint tenancy (explained in Chapter 4, Section C), is an excellent probate avoidance technique for couples and co-owners of personal and real property who want the surviving owner to inherit their share. Couples who buy a house or other valuable property often take title in joint tenancy, so that when one of them dies the other can get the property quickly and easily, and keep a significant portion of the estate out of probate.

Unfortunately, using joint tenancy as a probate avoidance technique for individually-owned property is often not a wise idea, for three reasons:

- Property transferred into joint tenancy with someone else cannot be called back if you change your mind. With a will, pay-on-death bank account, insurance policy or living trust, you are free to change your mind and give or leave the property to someone else.

- Property transferred to a joint tenant belongs to the new joint tenant as soon as the transfer is made. The new owner can sell or give away the property, or it can be taken by his or her creditors or by the government to pay unpaid taxes. In short, your efforts to transfer property to avoid probate fees later can cause you serious problems now.

- If the original property owner is elderly and transfers the property into joint tenancy with a younger person, there is always the possibility that the younger person will die first and full ownership of the property will revert to the older one. If, in the meantime, the elderly individual is no longer competent to make business decisions, the property is likely to pass under the residuary clause of a will and end up in probate after all.

▶ **Joint Tenancy in Community Property States**
▶ **(Arizona, California, Idaho, Nevada, New Mexico, Texas,**
▶ **Washington and Wisconsin)**
▶ Most married couples who live in states with community property laws prefer to
▶ take title to jointly-owned property as "community property" or as "community
▶ property held in joint tenancy." The reason for this is that under federal estate tax
▶ rules, both shares of community property are automatically entitled to a stepped-
▶ up tax basis upon the death of either spouse. This can be a significant tax break.
▶ By contrast, only the deceased spouse's half of jointly-owned property that is not
▶ community property qualifies for a stepped-up tax basis.
▶   Property held in the name of one spouse or in joint tenancy may legally be
▶ community property. If so, it will still qualify for a stepped-up tax basis. The
▶ problem is that when one spouse dies, the IRS presumes that property held in joint
▶ tenancy is not community property, and it is up to the surviving spouse to prove
▶ that it is.
▶   In California and some other community property states, if the deceased
▶ person's share of community property is left to the surviving spouse, it qualifies for
▶ a quick and easy summary probate procedure that can be processed without a
▶ lawyer. Nevertheless, because some paperwork and delay is still involved, some
▶ estate planning experts recommend holding property in joint tenancy to avoid
▶ probate, while carefully documenting that it was purchased with community
▶ property funds or otherwise transferred to community property ownership, to
▶ qualify for the stepped-up tax basis.

Revocable Living Trusts

A revocable living trust is a legal entity you create by preparing and signing a
document that looks fairly similar to a will. In the trust document, you specify
who you want to receive certain property at your death. Unlike property left in
a will, however, property subject to a living trust avoids the cost and delay of
probate.

Revocable living trusts are extremely flexible. You can leave all of your
property by living trust. Or, as commonly occurs, you can use a living trust to
leave only some assets—leaving the remainder by will or one or more of the
other probate avoidance techniques discussed in this chapter. Unlike wills,
living trusts are not made public at your death.

These trusts are called "living" or sometimes "inter vivos" (Latin for "among the living") because they are created while you're alive. They're called "revocable" because you can revoke or change them at any time, for any reason, before you die. During your lifetime, you still have control over all property transferred to your living trust and can do what you want with it—sell it, spend it, or give it away.

▶ ## Living Trust Technicalities

Living trusts are simple in concept. The person who establishes the trust—called in legalese either the "settlor," "grantor" or "creator"—signs a trust document that contains these elements:

1. A list of the property that is subject to the trust—for example, the house at 12 Marden Road, Purchase, New York and brokerage account 1278 at Racafrax Co.

2. The name of a "trustee," who has power to manage the trust property. Normally, the person who establishes the trust names himself or herself as trustee.

3. The names of the beneficiary or beneficiaries. These are the people who will receive the trust property at the creator's death.

4. The name of the "successor trustee" who will take over when the person who set up the trust dies and turn the trust property over to the beneficiaries. In most living trusts, the successor trustee is also given the power to manage the property if the creator becomes disabled. The successor trustee is often one of the trust's principal beneficiaries.

5. The terms of the trust. These always give the creator power to amend or revoke it at any time.

A living trust can transfer property to inheritors only if ownership of the property is transferred to the trust's name. Ownership documents—the title to your house, your securities, and your motor vehicle title slip—must be officially changed to the trust's name or the trust will not control the property.

One drawback of a living trust is the relatively small hassle of transferring ownership of property to the trust and conducting future personal business in the name of the trust. There may also be transfer taxes when you transfer property to the trust's name. Fortunately, there is no need to file a separate tax return for the trust. All transactions made by your living trust, such as the sale of property at a profit, are reported on your personal income tax return.

► **Self-Help for Living Trusts**
►
► You may be able to create a living trust without a lawyer's assistance by using one
► or more of these self-help tools:
►
► • *Nolo's Living Trust* by Mary Randolph (Nolo Press). Order information is at the
►   back of the manual.
►
► • *Plan Your Estate with a Living Trust* by Denis Clifford (Nolo Press). Order
►   information is at the back of the manual.

Who Should Have a Living Trust?

Despite its probate avoidance advantages compared with a will, a living trust
is not the best choice for everyone. As noted earlier, the amount of energy
you should expend on avoiding probate probably depends on your age,
health, the amount of property involved and the workiness of a particular
probate avoidance device. Here's a thumbnail outline of how to approach the
problem sensibly.

Age 70 or Over   Use a living trust for all or most valuable assets not covered
by other probate avoidance devices.

   Exception   Married couples in community property states such as
California, whose property is all community property and who want the
survivor to inherit everything, may conclude it is unnecessary to go through
hoops to avoid probate. Community property left to a surviving spouse can
already pass through simplified probate.

Age 60 or under, in good health   Many people in this group conclude that
they can get along fine for a while by using a will, coupled with some of the
easier probate avoidance techniques, such as owning their house in joint
tenancy or placing a pay-on-death designation on bank and retirement
accounts. In this age group, with a normal life expectancy of at least 25 years,
the time and trouble necessary to maintain a living trust for many years may
be considerable.

   Exception   People with estates worth more than $500,000 will likely
conclude that placing a few of their most valuable assets in a living trust
makes sense. For example, a business or real property not already held in joint

tenancy could be transferred to a living trust while other assets are disposed of by a will.

Age 60–70 The older you get, the more sense it makes to plan to avoid probate on all or most of your estate. A revocable living trust is often the most comprehensive way to accomplish this.

Can a Living Trust Replace a Will?

Even if you use a living trust to pass all of your identifiable property, there are several reasons why you need a will, too:

- You can't nominate a personal guardian for minor children in a living trust—you need a will. (See Chapter 7, Section C.)

- A living trust works to pass only property you transfer to the trust's name. Property you may receive in the future, but do not have title to now, cannot be transferred by living trust. For example, if you have inherited property that is still tied up in probate, or you expect to receive money from the settlement of a lawsuit, you need a will. And because you cannot accurately predict what property you might receive shortly before death, it is advisable to back up a living trust with a will.

C. Federal Estate Taxes

The first $600,000 you leave at your death or give away while you are alive is exempt from federal estate tax. This means that if your estate is worth less than $600,000, and you haven't already given away large amounts, you need not worry about federal estate taxes. However, if you have an estate larger than $600,000, or if you are married and plan to leave your property to your spouse, who will then have an estate exceeding $600,000, please read on.

This section helps you estimate your federal estate tax liability. Section D discusses what you can do to keep your tax bill to a minimum. Be aware that if an estate is large enough to be taxed, federal estate taxes are hefty. They begin at 37% for property valued between $600,000 to $750,000 and increase gradually for larger estates—topping out at 55% for estates larger than $3,000,000.[2]

1. Estimate the Value of Your Net Estate

Your net worth is all you own less all you owe (assets minus liabilities).[3] If you are married or co-own property with another person, be careful to distinguish between your property and your spouse's (or other owner's) when computing your net worth. For example, if you and your spouse own a house in joint tenancy, include only half of your combined equity when computing your net worth.

Example

If you own a house worth $350,000 with a $100,000 mortgage, it's worth $250,000 for estate tax purposes. If you and your spouse or any other co-owner own the house in equal shares, your share is only $125,000.

---

[2] *Plan Your Estate: Wills, Probate Avoidance, Trusts and Taxes* by Denis Clifford (Nolo Press) deals with these issues in more detail.

[3] Nolo's *For the Record* computer program has a feature that computes your net worth based on the fair market value of your equity interest in all property recorded in the program.

▶
▶
▶ **Marital Property: Who Owns What?**
▶ Here is a brief outline of marital property ownership laws.
▶ (A more thorough explanation is contained in Chapter 4, Section C.)
▶
▶ **Community Property States**
▶
▶ Arizona   Nevada   Washington
▶ California   New Mexico   Wisconsin
▶ Idaho   Texas
▶
▶ All property either spouse earns or acquires during marriage is community
▶ property, jointly owned by both, with several exceptions. The most important is
▶ that the gifts or inheritances of one spouse are that person's separately-owned
▶ property. All property acquired by one spouse before marriage is also separate
▶ property.
▶
▶ **Other States**
▶
▶ In all other states, the person whose name is on the ownership (title) document for
▶ a particular piece of property owns it for estate tax purposes. If both names are on
▶ the document, ownership is joint. Property with no title document belongs to the
▶ spouse who used his or her money to purchase it, unless it was a gift to the other.
▶

2. Deduct Allowable Estate Tax Exemptions

Federal law exempts certain property from estate tax, including:

- up to $600,000 left to any beneficiaries;

- all property left to your spouse;

- all property left to tax-exempt charitable organizations; and

- amounts paid for last illness, burial and probate costs.

The $600,000 Exemption

Property you own at your death worth up to $600,000 is exempt from federal
estate tax. This is true no matter what type of property is involved, to whom
you leave it and the legal device used to transfer it—will, living trust or joint
tenancy.

Example

Bruce leaves his estate of $700,000 to his son. $100,000 is subject to federal estate tax. This is true whether he uses a will, a living trust or another transfer device.

There is an important qualification to this rule. Gifts made during life—if worth over $10,000 per year per person and not made to a tax-exempt charity—count toward the $600,000 exempt amount. The federal government feared that if large gifts were not taxed at the same rate as property left at death, people with estates large enough to be taxed would simply give the bulk of their property away shortly before death. The result of this fear is a unified system of estate and gift taxes. It works like this. If you make a taxable gift during your life, you must file a gift tax return, but you don't pay tax then. Instead, the amount of the gift that exceeds $10,000 per person is subtracted from your $600,000.

Example

Clint gives his son Larry and daughter-in-law Glenda $30,000 for the downpayment on a house. Since $10,000 can be given to an individual each year free of any gift tax consequences, only $10,000 is taxable. But no gift tax is due. The $10,000 is subtracted from the $600,000 lifetime estate and gift tax exemption. Had John wanted to avoid tax altogether, he could have given Larry and Glenda $20,000 in one calendar year and $10,000 the next year.

Property Left to Your Spouse

All property left to a surviving spouse, whether it's worth $10 or $10 million, is exempt from federal estate tax.[4] In tax lingo, this exemption is called the "marital deduction."

Example

Sue has an estate valued at $6,600,000. She leaves $600,000 to her children and $6,000,000 to her husband. All of Sue's property is estate tax-exempt. The $6,000,000 is exempt as a result of the marital deduction, and the remaining $600,000 is exempt under the standard $600,000 exemption discussed above.

---

[4]This exemption does not apply if the surviving spouse is not a U.S. citizen.

Often, however, you won't want to simply pile up all the money in the surviving spouse's estate. Alternatives are discussed in Section D(3) below.

Unmarried Couples Note: There are no estate tax exemptions similar to the marital deduction for lovers or roommates.[5] However, the marital deduction is available for couples who entered into a common law marriage in one of the 14 states that recognize this type of marriage. (See Chapter 3, Section B.) It is also available to people who marry very shortly before dying.

Charitable Gift Exemption

All bequests made to tax-exempt charitable organizations are exempt from federal estate taxes; they don't need to be subtracted from the $600,000 exemption. If you plan to make large charitable bequests to an organization, doublecheck its tax-exemption status. The normal way an organization becomes a tax-exempt charity is by a favorable ruling from the IRS, under Internal Revenue Code Section 501(c)(3). Organizations that are active politically—a term not consistently defined by the IRS—are often not tax-exempt.

Other Estate Tax Exemptions and Credits

The other principal exemptions from federal estate tax and estate tax credits are:

- expenses of last illness, burial costs and probate costs; and
- a tax credit for money paid for state estate and inheritance taxes, and taxes imposed by foreign countries on property owned there. A few states have no estate or inheritance taxes. A second, larger group levies a small "pick-up" tax calculated to equal the maximum amount that can be credited

---

[5]Perhaps there is a certain perverse fairness in this, as unmarried couples normally receive significant income tax benefits if both have income. For a thorough discussion of the legal rights and responsibilities of unmarried couples, see *The Living Together Kit,* Warner and Ihara (Nolo Press), and *A Legal Guide for Lesbian and Gay Couples,* Curry and Clifford (Nolo Press).

against federal estate taxes. Other states, especially in the northeast, levy substantial death taxes on large estates. If your estate pays these, it will receive a small credit on your federal estate tax. (See Section D, below.)

3. Estimate Your Estate Tax

You are now ready to broadly estimate your tax liability. Do so by consulting the rates shown in the table below. The example that follows will help you understand how to estimate your tax.

Unified Federal Estate and Gift Tax Rates[6]

Column A	Column B	Column C	Column D
Net taxable estate over	Net taxable estate not over	Tax on amount in column A	Rate of tax on excess over amount in column A
$ 0	$10,000	$ 0	18 %
10,000	20,000	1,800	20
20,000	40,000	3,800	22
40,000	60,000	8,200	24
60,000	80,000	13,000	26
80,000	100,000	18,200	28
100,000	150,000	23,800	30
150,000	250,000	38,800	32
250,000	500,000	70,800	34
500,000	750,000	155,800	37
750,000	1,000,000	248,300	39
1,000,000	1,250,000	345,800	41
1,250,000	1,500,000	448,300	43
1,500,000	2,000,000	555,800	45
2,000,000	2,500,000	780,800	49
2,500,000	3,000,000	1,025,800	53
3,000,000	infinity		55

[6]In looking at this chart, remember that, outside of gifts of $10,000 or more to one individual, $600,000 is exempt from federal estate tax.

Example 1

Bernie, a resident of California, anticipates that after subtracting liabilities from assets and then subtracting exempt amounts, including charitable gifts and funeral costs, his estate's value is about $1.5 million. Bernie plans to leave $500,000 to his spouse and $1 million to his children and other beneficiaries. All property Bernie leaves to his spouse is exempt from federal estate tax because of the marital deduction. This means his net estate subject to tax is $1 million. Column C on the Estate Tax Chart reveals that the tax assessed on a $1 million estate is $345,800. Because $600,000 of that amount isn't taxed, he subtracts $192,800—the tax assessed against a $600,000 estate. Bernie's estate will have to pay federal taxes of $153,000.[7]

Incidentally, Bernie is an excellent candidate to give money to his kids while he is still alive. By doing this, he can reduce the size of his estate and therefore the tax. (See Section D1.)

D. Reducing Federal Estate Taxes

Unfortunately, aside from leaving more money to your spouse or to charity, there are only a few major ways to lower estate taxes.

1. Give Away Property While You're Alive

An excellent way to reduce your estate tax liability is to reduce the size of your estate by giving property to the same people or organizations you would leave it to. But, if you make large gifts—more than $10,000 per person or organization per year—you accomplish nothing, because the amount of the gift over $10,000 is subtracted from your total $600,000 exemption. The key is to make a number of smaller gifts.

- Annually, you can give away property worth $10,000 or less per person or organization tax-free.

- A couple can give $20,000 a year tax-free to one person and $40,000 to another couple.

---

[7]Bernie's estate would also be liable to pay state inheritance taxes. California takes some of the tax assessed by the federal government; it doesn't impose any extra tax.

- All gifts to tax-exempt nonprofits are exempt from gift and estate tax.
- This strategy can be repeated year after year.

Gift-giving to reduce estate tax liability works well for people who have enough property that they can afford to be generous. It is particularly advantageous for reasonably affluent people who have several children, grandchildren or other objects of their affection.

Gifts of Appreciated Property Shortly Before Death

Someone who inherits property gets a "stepped-up" tax basis in the property to its then-current market value. Because the tax basis is the number used to figure capital gains and losses, this means an inheritor who promptly sells property for its fair market value pays no capital gains tax. However, property given away keeps the giver's tax basis—purchase price plus any capital improvements. Thus, in the case of greatly appreciated property, a person who receives it by gift faces a much larger tax bill when it's sold than does someone who inherits it.

Example

Ellen gives a 100-acre parcel of undeveloped land to her son John shortly before she dies. Since Ellen's tax basis in the land at the time of transfer was $100,000, this is now John's tax basis. If John sells the land for $500,000, he owes capital gains tax on $400,000. By contrast, had Ellen left John the property at death, his tax basis would have been "stepped-up" to $500,000, fair market value, and no tax would have been due had he sold it for that amount.

Gifts of Life Insurance

Life insurance policies you own on your own life and give away at least three years before your death make good gifts from an estate planning vantage. Potential tax liability is assessed on the present value of the insurance policy, which is far less than the amount the policy will pay off at death. Indeed, in many instances, it will be less than the $10,000 annual tax exclusion for gifts.

▶ To give away a life insurance policy, you must carefully follow fairly technical
▶ IRS rules, which should be available from your insurance company. Basically, you
▶ must make an irrevocable gift of the policy. If you keep the right to revoke the
▶ gift—that is, get the policy back—it will be taxed as part of your estate. If you
▶ prepay the entire policy with a single premium, giving it away creates no future
▶ payment problems. However, if you purchase a policy that requires annual
▶ premiums, the person you give it to must make future payments, which may mean
▶ you'll want to make annual gifts large enough to cover the payments.

Example

Bert has an estate worth $1 million. He purchases three single-premium life insurance policies for $50,000 each and immediately transfers ownership of the policies to his three children. Tax will be assessed on $120,000—the $150,000 value of the policies minus the $10,000 annual tax exemption for each gift. No gift tax need be paid at the time of transfer—the $120,000 is subtracted from the unified $600,000 estate and gift tax exemption, leaving $480,000 for use at death.

The policies pay off $200,000 each at Bert's death ten years later. Bert has transferred $600,000 to his children, but only $120,000 will be part of his taxable estate. Had he kept the policy because he wanted to borrow against it, or for some other reason, his estate would owe tax on the entire $600,000 of proceeds.

2. Generation-Skipping Trusts

Creating a "generation-skipping" trust for the benefit of your grandchildren won't reduce your own estate tax liability; it can, however, exempt up to $1 million from tax in the next generation. A generation-skipping trust, as the name indicates, leaves property in trust for beneficiaries two generations removed from the trust creator—normally, your grandchildren. For example, if you leave $1 million in trust for your grandchildren, with the income from the trust available to your children, that $1 million is excluded from your children's taxable estate when they die. (See Chapter 7, Section D for more information on trusts for grandchildren.)

3. Create a Marital Life Estate Trust

Spouses who have a combined estate of more than $600,000 and who are both elderly should usually avoid leaving large sums to one another. This is because the survivor's estate will have to pay a much larger estate tax than if the other spouse had left the property directly to the children or other beneficiaries.

One way to avoid this problem, and also provide some income for the surviving spouse, is for each spouse to leave the other property in a "marital life estate trust"—sometimes called a "spousal trust" or "A-B trust." With this kind of trust, the income goes to the survivor during his or her life, and the principal goes to named beneficiaries (often the children) when the second spouse dies. It allows you to avoid increasing the size of your spouse's estate.

The main drawback of a marital life estate trust is that the surviving spouse receives only the income from the money or property placed in trust— or the use of the property if it's tangible, such as a house. He or she does not own it.[8] Obviously, for a spouse who already has more than enough property, this is not a problem. However, marital life estate trusts are generally not desirable for younger couples because should one die, the other spouse, who will likely live for many years, will want to own the property outright.

Example

Calvin and Phyllis, husband and wife, are each in their mid-70s, and each has an estate worth $450,000. Calvin dies, leaving all his property to Phyllis. Because of the marital deduction, no estate tax is assessed. Phyllis dies the next year. Her estate consists of the entire $900,000 (plus any appreciation), which she leaves to the children. Because $600,000 can be left to anyone free of estate tax, $300,000 of the money left to the children is subject to tax. Unfortunately, however, it is taxed at the hefty marginal rate of 39%.

If Calvin and Phyllis had each established a marital life estate trust, with the income to go to the survivor for life and the principal to the children at the survivor's death, there would be no estate tax liability.

---

[8]The surviving spouse can, at the option of the trust creator, be given the right to spend trust principal for medical needs and other basic necessities.

E. State Death Taxes

About half the states impose death taxes on:

- all real estate owned in the state, no matter where the deceased lived; and
- all other property of state residents, no matter where it's located.

If you reside in a state that does not impose death taxes—and do not own any real property in one that does—skip to section F.

▸ **States Without Death Taxes**[9]

Alabama	Hawaii	Oregon
Alaska	Illinois	Texas
Arizona	Maine	Utah
Arkansas	Minnesota	Vermont
California	Missouri	Virginia
Colorado	Nevada	Washington
District of Columbia	New Mexico	West Virginia
Florida	North Dakota	Wyoming
Georgia		

1. What State Will Tax You?

State death taxes are imposed on all those who reside in the state permanently. If you divide your time between states, you'll probably want to establish your residence in the one with the lower tax rate. (See Chapter 3, Section B, for a discussion of legal residence.)

---

[9]Many of these states charge a small "pick-up" tax equal to the amount of the federal tax credit for state inheritance taxes, but the result is no net tax.

Example

James and Vivian, a retired couple, divide the year between Florida and their native New York. Florida effectively has no death taxes. New York imposes comparatively stiff taxes—with rates ranging from 2% for $50,000 or less to 21% for $100,000 or more. Other things being equal, it makes sense for them to officially reside in Florida. To establish this, they should scrupulously maintain all their major business contacts in Florida, including registering all vehicles in that state and maintaining bank accounts there. In addition, they should vote there. And because real property is taxed in the state where it's located (regardless of its owner's residence), they might consider selling any New York real property and renting there instead.

 Establishing residence in a no-tax state can sometimes be tricky if you also live in a high-tax one part of the year, because the high-tax state has an interest in concluding that you really reside there. If you find yourself in this situation and have a large estate, check your plan with a knowledgeable tax lawyer or accountant.

2. Estate Planning for State Death Taxes

In many instances, the bite taken out of estates by state death taxes is annoying, but relatively minor—especially when property is left to a spouse or children. But tax liability can be significant for property given to non-relatives. For example, Nebraska imposes a 15% death tax rate if $25,000 is given to a friend, but only 1% if it is given to a spouse. It is probably rare that someone would change the amount of property left to a beneficiary because of the impact of state death taxes, but you should at least be aware of them.[10]

---

[10]Death tax rules for all states that impose them are summarized in *Plan Your Estate,* by Denis Clifford (Nolo Press). More detailed information is available from your state tax officials.

F. Estate Planning to Control Property

Most people are content to leave their property to their inheritors outright, and not try to control what they do with it. However, there are times, especially for people with larger estates, when it can make sense to impose controls on what inheritors can do with property. The most common situations are discussed here.

1. Money Left to Minor Children and Young Adults

As discussed in Chapter 7, many people who leave property to minor children, either as first choice or alternate beneficiaries, want to delay the age beyond 18 at which the beneficiaries will receive the property.

2. Property Left to Children of Previous Marriages

People in second or subsequent marriages who have children from a previous marriage often want some or all of their estate to be left for the benefit of their current spouse, but want the property to pass eventually to the children. To take care of this concern—and for estates larger than $600,000, to simultaneously save on federal estate taxes—each spouse should leave their property in a marital trust. (See Section D3, above).

3. Money Left in Managerial Trusts

If a beneficiary will need long-term help with property management, you may want to establish a managerial trust that is carefully tailored to meet the complicated needs of the beneficiary.

 See a lawyer with experience in this area in your state for help in drafting a managerial trust.

Trusts for People Who Can't Manage Money

If you want to leave property to a financially improvident adult in a way that prevents him or her from spending it all at once, a spendthrift trust, in which a trusted person or institution is empowered to dole out the money little by little, is a good idea.

Trusts for Disadvantaged Persons

A person with a physical or mental disability may not be able to handle property, no matter what age. The solution is often to establish a trust with a reliable adult as trustee to manage the disabled person's trust property. This is similar in concept to a spendthrift trust, but a trust for a disadvantaged person should be constructed to take full advantage of funds available from public sources.

Trusts for a Group of Beneficiaries

For a variety of reasons, someone may choose that the specific plan for how his or her estate is distributed should be determined after he or she dies instead of during life. The usual way to accomplish this is to create what is called a "sprinkling trust," in legal parlance. Normally, the trust creator names the beneficiaries of the trust during life, but does not divide the property among them. That is done by the trustee, after the creator dies, under whatever general criteria the trust sets forth.

G. Planning for Incapacity

Although, strictly speaking, it's not estate planning, it is sensible to prepare for the contingency that you may become incapacitated and can no longer handle your own financial affairs or make medical decisions.

1. Durable Powers of Attorney

One way to plan for incapacity is to prepare two documents called durable powers of attorney. In one, you appoint someone, called your "attorney in fact," to manage your financial and business affairs if you cannot. In the other, you appoint someone else to make health care decisions should you become incapacitated—including whether to prolong your life artificially with life support equipment. Nearly half the states now have laws recognizing and regulating durable powers of attorney for health care.

Normally, neither durable power of attorney is designed to take effect unless and until you become incapacitated. Each functions as a kind of insurance that someone of your choice will manage your affairs and make crucial decisions about your finances, comfort, health and even your life if you become incapacitated.

2. Living Wills

A living will is not a will at all—and not appropriate to consider as part of a will. Living wills take effect during your lifetime, as a way to direct medical care; a will takes effect at your death, as a way to direct disposition of your property.

Sometimes called a Directive to Physicians or Advanced Directive, a living will is presently directed to a doctor, hospital or other medical provider. If you wish, it becomes part of your official medical record, legally binding the physician or hospital to follow your wishes about life-sustaining or other types of treatment should you become incapacitated. Some states permit a living will to name another person, a "proxy," to make medical decisions on behalf of an incapacitated patient. Most states now permit living wills, although the laws vary—with the heavy restriction in some that a living will is legally binding only if it is signed after you are diagnosed with a terminal disease.

▶ It Is Best To Prepare Both Documents

People directing their own decisions about life-sustaining medical care is a fairly novel concept—and courts are still settling the legal effect of documents intended to do so. If you want to have the best chance to ensure that your wishes for medical care are followed, it is best to prepare both a durable power of attorney for medical care and a living will. But make sure the two are consistent. Your attorney-in-fact for health care should be the same person as the proxy named in your living will. The language used to direct your medical treatment should also be the same.

3. Living Trusts

A living trust, which is often recommended as an estate planning device, can also be used to plan for the possibility that you will be unable to handle your own affairs. In the document that creates the trust, you can empower the successor trustee—the person who takes over when you die—to manage your affairs should you become incapacitated. However, a living trust is not an adequate substitute for a durable power of attorney for financial affairs because a successor trustee has power only over property transferred to the trust—not over other assets or income you may receive from pensions and other sources. And the successor trustee is not authorized to make medical decisions on your behalf. (For more information on living trusts, see *Plan Your Estate with a Living Trust* by Denis Clifford and *Nolo's Living Trust,* a software package by Mary Randolph. Both are published by Nolo Press.)

14 If You Need Expert Help

Experience has shown that most WillMaker users do not need a lawyer's help. The issues involved in making a basic will are normally straightforward and easy to understand.

The same goes for basic estate planning to avoid probate and save on estate taxes. If your estate is worth less than $1 million and you have a book such as Nolo's *Plan Your Estate*, you probably won't need more help.

Legal questions can arise, however, for which you will want to see an expert—especially if you have a very large estate, must plan for an incapacitated minor, or have to deal with the assets of a small business.

A. What Kind of Expert Do You Need?

The first question to decide if you want to consult an expert is what type you need. Here are a few suggestions:

- A financial planner is probably your best bet if you want to integrate planning into the rest of your life—including your retirement with your estate plan. This involves looking at a number of variables such as how much you are saving, the most suitable type of investments given your age and family structure, expected retirement income and insurance needs.

- A certified public accountant (CPA) is most appropriate if you are primarily concerned about determining federal and state death tax liability. If you conclude that you will need a trust or other legal document drafted, this may mean you will also need to consult an attorney; but it is usually best, and less expensive, to start with a CPA.

- A lawyer is most appropriate if you have questions about drafting a will, or a probate-avoiding living trust or a more sophisticated trust designed to save on federal estate taxes or to provide extensive management for a beneficiary who cannot handle assets on his or her own.

B. Types of Lawyers

Assuming that you or a financial or tax expert has concluded that you need to consult with a lawyer, you must then decide what type of lawyer is right for you and your situation. At the risk of oversimplifying, you have two choices: an attorney in general practice or an estate planning specialist. Expect to pay a specialist up to 50% more than a general practitioner.

Making a choice as to which you need is most often a matter of common sense. If you want a completed WillMaker will reviewed, or need an answer to a specific question such what effect an out-of-the-country divorce may have on your willmaking plans, a general practitioner is adequate.

However, if your estate is large—worth $1 million or more—and you want to plan to minimize estate taxes, or you need a trust to provide management for a mentally disadvantaged beneficiary or to provide a life estate for a surviving spouse, you should see a specialist.

C. Where to Look for a Lawyer

Finding a competent lawyer who charges a reasonable fee and respects your efforts to prepare your own will may not be easy. Especially when it comes to being involved in making your own untrained decisions and drafting your own will, many lawyers will instinctively react with barely-disguised hostility. But like all generalizations, this one has exceptions. Lawyers who will work willingly and well with people who want to be actively involved in their own legal lives do exist. Here are some suggestions on how to find one:

1. Ask Friends and Business Associates

Almost anyone running a small business has a relationship with a lawyer. Ask around to find someone you know who has been satisfied with a lawyer's services. If that lawyer does not handle estate planning, he or she will likely know someone who does. And because of the continuing relationship with your friend, the lawyer making the referral has an incentive to recommend someone who is competent. These days, most urban areas have a number of lawyers who specialize in estate planning, so if you want a specialist, you don't need to settle for a friend of a friend who does an occasional will.

Also ask people you know in any political or social organization in which you are involved. They may know of a competent lawyer whose attitudes are similar to yours. Senior citizen centers and other groups that advise and assist older people are particularly likely to have a list of local lawyers who specialize in wills and estate planning and who are generally regarded as competent and caring.

2. Look Into a Group Legal Plan

Some unions, employers and consumer action organizations offer group legal plans to their members or employees, who can obtain comprehensive legal assistance free or for low rates. If you are a member of such a plan, check with it first. Your problem may be covered free of charge. But if the plan gives you only a slight reduction in a lawyer's fee, as many do, keep in mind that you may be referred to a lawyer whose main virtue is the willingness to reduce fees in exchange for a high volume of referrals.

3. Check Out a Prepaid Legal Plan

Prepaid legal plans are sold by companies such as Bank of America, Montgomery Ward and Amway, and are often offered to credit card holders or sold door-to-door. They typically offer the subscriber the right to have simple questions answered, letters written or a straightforward will drafted. Often, the will that comes with the plan is less sophisticated than WillMaker's, so there is little reason to consult one of these plans merely to draft a simple will. The basic fee in most plans will rarely cover more sophisticated estate planning, but of course, plan lawyers will usually be happy to sell you their time and expertise.

Unfortunately, there's no guarantee that the lawyers available through these plans are of the best caliber. In fact, competent, busy lawyers rarely join these plans because they already have enough business. As with any consumer transaction, if you do go the prepaid route, check out the plan and the lawyer to whom you are referred to—before signing up.

Whenever you avail yourself of any service offered by these prepaid insurance plans, be forewarned: The lawyer you see receives at most $2 or $3 for dealing with you, and may have agreed to this minimal amount in the hope of finding clients who will pay for extra legal services not covered by the monthly premium. For example, some plans that offer a will for no charge beyond the original membership fee charge hundreds of dollars extra if you want to include a simple children's trust such as the one included in the WillMaker will. So, if the plan lawyer recommends an expensive legal procedure rather than a simple will or probate avoidance device such as a living trust, get a second opinion.

4. Consult a Law Clinic

Law clinics such as Hyatt Legal Services and Jacoby & Meyers loudly advertise their low initial consultation fees. This generally means that a basic consultation is cheap (often about $20); anything beyond that isn't so cheap. Generally, the rates are about the same as those charged by the average lawyer in general practice.

What is not advertised is that most clinics have extremely high lawyer turnover and, as a result, it can be difficult to form a long-term relationship with a lawyer. This may be fine if you want a simple question answered. However, if you want a lawyer to help you draft a fairly complicated estate plan and then be available over the years to redraft it a number of times as your needs change, a legal clinic is probably a poor choice.

5. Call an Attorney Referral Service

Most county bar associations maintain referral services that will give you the name of an attorney who practices in your area. Usually you can get a referral to an attorney who claims to specialize in wills and will give you an initial consultation for a low fee. A problem with these services is that they usually provide minimal screening for the attorneys listed, which means those who participate may not be the most experienced or competent. It may be possible to find a skilled estate planning specialist following this approach, but be sure to take the time to check out the credentials and experience of the person to whom you're referred.

6. Read the Classified Ads

Check the classified ads under "Attorneys." There are quite a few attorneys around who are no longer interested in handling court-contested matters but do provide consultations at relatively low rates. This could be just what you need—especially if yours is a fairly basic question.

D. Dealing with a Lawyer

It is no secret that lawyers are expensive. Their fees usually range from $100 to $400 or more per hour. While fancy office trappings and designer suits are no indication that a lawyer will provide top-notch service in a style with which you will feel comfortable, these conventional trappings usually ensure rates at the upper end of the scale.

Once you have concluded on the basis of a reliable referral that a particular lawyer is probably competent, your next job is to check his or her attitude. People who use self-help tools such as WillMaker typically expect professionals to help educate them to make their own informed decisions—not to treat them as a traditional, obedient client. Such a match may be difficult to find.

Most important, be sure you've settled your fee arrangement—in writing—at the start of your relationship. Depending on the area of the county where you live, generally, fees of $100 to $150 per hour are reasonable for a general practice lawyer. Experienced specialists are likely to charge closer to $200 per hour. In addition to the hourly fee, you should get a clear, written commitment from the lawyer concerning how many hours it is likely to take to resolve your problem.

Finally, ask the lawyer several specific questions about your problem. Do you get clear, concise answers? If not, try someone else. If the lawyer acts wise but says little except to ask that the problem be placed in his or her hands—with a substantial fee, of course—watch out. You're either dealing with the common complication of someone who doesn't know the answer and won't admit it or someone who finds it impossible to let go of the "me expert, you plebeian" philosophy—even more common.

INDEX

CATALOG

SELF-HELP LAW BOOKS & SOFTWARE

ESTATE PLANNING & PROBATE

Plan Your Estate With a Living Trust

Attorney Denis Clifford
National 2nd Edition
This book covers every significant aspect of estate planning and gives detailed specific, instructions for preparing a living trust, a document that lets your family avoid expensive and lengthy probate court proceedings after your death. *Plan Your Estate* includes all the tear-out forms and step-by-step instructions to let you prepare an estate plan designed for your special needs.
$19.95/NEST

Nolo's Simple Will Book

Attorney Denis Clifford
National 2nd Edition
It's easy to write a legally valid will using this book. The instructions and forms enable people to draft a will for all needs, including naming a personal guardian for minor children, leaving property to minor children or young adults and updating a will when necessary. Good in all states except Louisiana.
$17.95/SWIL

The Conservatorship Book

Lisa Goldoftas & Attorney Carolyn Farren
California 1st Edition
When someone becomes incapacitated due to illness or age, a conservator may need to take charge of their medical and financial affairs. *The Conservatorship Book* comes with complete instructions and all the forms necessary to file conservatorship documents, appear in court, be appointed conservator and end a conservatorship.
$24.95/CNSV

How to Probate an Estate

Julia Nissley
California 6th Edition
If you find yourself responsible for winding up the legal and financial affairs of a deceased family member or friend, you can often save costly attorneys' fees by handling the probate process yourself. This book also explains the simple procedures you can use to transfer assets that don't require probate, including property held in joint tenancy or living trusts or as community property.
$34.95/PAE

software

WillMaker

Nolo Press
Version 4.0
This easy-to-use software program lets you prepare and update a legal will—safely, privately and without the expense of a lawyer. Leading you step-by-step in a question-and-answer format, *WillMaker* builds a will around your answers, taking into account your state of residence. *WillMaker* comes with a 200-page legal manual which provides the legal background necessary to make sound choices. Good in all states except Louisiana.
IBM PC
(31/2 & 51/4 disks included)
$69.95/WI4
MACINTOSH $69.95/WM4

Nolo's Personal RecordKeeper

(formerly For the Record)
Carol Pladsen & Attorney Ralph Warner
Version 3.0
Nolo's Personal RecordKeeper lets you record the location of personal, financial and legal information in over 200 categories and subcategories. It also allows you to create lists of insured property, compute net worth, consolidate emergency information into one place and export to *Quicken*® home inventory and net worth reports. Includes a 320-page manual filled with practical and legal advice.
IBM PC
(3-1/2 & 5-1/4 disks included)
$49.95/FRI3
MACINTOSH $49.95/FRM3

Nolo's Living Trust

Attorney Mary Randolph
Version 1.0
A will is an indispensable part of any estate plan, but many people need a living trust as well. By putting certain assets into a trust, you save your heirs the headache, time and expense of probate. *Nolo's Living Trust* lets you set up an individual or shared marital trust, make your trust document legal, transfer your property to the trust, and change or revoke the trust at any time. The 380-page manual guides you through the process step-by-step, and over 100 legal help screens and an on-line glossary explain key legal terms and concepts. Good in all states except Louisiana.
MACINTOSH $79.95/LTM1

Everybody's Guide to Municipal Court

Judge Roderic Duncan
California 1st Edition
Everybody's Guide to Municipal Court explains how to prepare and defend the most common types of contract and personal injury law suits in California Municipal Court. Written by a California judge, the book provides step-by-step instructions for preparing and filing all necessary forms, gathering evidence and appearing in court.
$29.95/MUNI

Fight Your Ticket

Attorney David Brown
California 5th Edition
This book shows you how to fight an unfair traffic ticket—when you're stopped, at arraignment, at trial and on appeal.
$17.95/FYT

Collect Your Court Judgment

Gini Graham Scott, Attorney Stephen Elias & Lisa Goldoftas
California 2nd Edition
This book contains step-by-step instructions and all the forms you need to collect a court judgment from the debtor's bank accounts, wages, business receipts, real estate or other assets.
$19.95/JUDG

How to Change Your Name

Attorneys David Loeb & David Brown
California 5th Edition
This book explains how to change your name legally and provides all the necessary court forms with detailed instructions on how to fill them out.
$19.95/NAME

Everybody's Guide to Small Claims Court

Attorney Ralph Warner
National 5th Edition
California 10th Edition
These books will help you decide if you should sue in Small Claims Court, show you how to file and serve papers, tell you what to bring to court and how to collect a judgment.
National $15.95/NSCC
California $15.95/ CSCC

The Criminal Records Book

Attorney Warren Siegel
California 3rd Edition
This book shows you step-by-step how to seal criminal records, dismiss convictions, destroy marijuana records and reduce felony convictions.
$19.95/CRIM

Legal Breakdown: 40 Ways to Fix Our Legal System

Nolo Press Editors and Staff
National 1st Edition
Legal Breakdown presents 40 common-sense proposals to make our legal system fairer, faster, cheaper and more accessible. It advocates abolishing probate, taking divorce out of court, treating jurors better and a host of other fundamental changes.
$8.95/LEG

The Legal Guide for Starting & Running a Small Business

Attorney Fred S. Steingold
National 1st Edition
This book is an essential resource for every small business owner, whether you are just starting out or are already established.
Find out everything you need to know about how to form a sole proprietorship, partnership or corporation, negotiate a favorable lease, hire and fire employees, write contracts and resolve business. disputes.
$19.95 / RUNS

Sexual Harassment on the Job

Attorneys William Petrocelli & Barbara Kate Repa
National 1st Edition
This is the first comprehensive book dealing with sexual harassment in the workplace. It describes what harassment is, what the laws are that make it illegal and how to put a stop to it. This guide is invaluable both for employees experiencing harassment and for employers interested in creating a policy against sexual harassment and a procedure for handling complaints.
$14.95/HARS

Your Rights in the Workplace

Dan Lacey
National 1st Edition
Your Rights in the Workplace, the first comprehensive guide to workplace rights—from hiring to firing—explains the latest sweeping changes in laws passed to protect workers. Learning about these legal protections can help all workers be sure they're paid fairly and on time, get all employment benefits, and know how to take action if fired or laid off illegally.
$15.95/YRW

How to Write a Business Plan
Mike McKeever
National 4th Edition
If you're thinking of starting a business or raising money to expand an existing one, this book will show you how to write the business plan and loan package necessary to finance your business and make it work.
$19.95/SBS

Marketing Without Advertising
Michael Phillips & Salli Rasberry
National 1st Edition
This book outlines practical steps for building and expanding a small business without spending a lot of money on advertising.
$14.00/MWAD

The Partnership Book
Attorneys Denis Clifford & Ralph Warner
National 4th Edition
This book shows you step-by-step how to write a solid partnership agreement that meets your needs. It covers initial contributions to the business, wages, profit-sharing, buyouts, death or retirement of a partner and disputes.
$24.95/PART

How to Form Your Own Nonprofit Corporation
Attorney Anthony Mancuso
National 1st Edition
This book explains the legal formalities involved and provides detailed information on the differences in the law among 50 states. It also contains forms for the Articles, Bylaws and Minutes you need, along with complete instructions for obtaining federal 501 (c) (3) tax exemptions and qualifying for public charity status.
$24.95/NNP

The California Nonprofit Corporation Handbook
Attorney Anthony Mancuso
California 6th Edition
This book shows you step-by-step how to form and operate a nonprofit corporation in California. It includes the latest corporate and tax law changes, and the forms for the Articles, Bylaws and Minutes.
$29.95/NON

How to Form Your Own Corporation
Attorney Anthony Mancuso
California 7th Edition
New York 2nd Edition
Texas 4th Edition
Florida 3rd Edition
These books contain the forms, instructions and tax information you need to incorporate a small business yourself and save hundreds of dollars in lawyers' fees.
California $29.95/CCOR
New York $24.95/NYCO
Texas $29.95/TCOR
Florida $24.95/FLCO

The California Professional Corporation Handbook
Attorney Anthony Mancuso
California 4th Edition
Health care professionals, lawyers, accountants and members of certain other professions must fulfill special requirements when forming a corporation in California. This book contains up-to-date tax information plus all the forms and instructions necessary to form a California professional corporation.
$34.95/PROF

The Independent Paralegal's Handbook
Attorney Ralph Warner
National 2nd Edition
The Independent Paralegal's Handbook provides legal and business guidelines for those who want to take routine legal work out of the law office and offer it for a reasonable fee in an independent business.
$19.95/ PARA

Getting Started as an Independent Paralegal
(Two Audio Tapes)
Attorney Ralph Warner
National 2nd Edition
If you are interested in going into business as an Independent Paralegal —helping consumers prepare their own legal paperwork in uncontested proceedings such as bankruptcy, divorce, small business incorporation, landlord-tenant actions and probate—you'll want to listen to these tapes. Approximately two hours in length, the tapes will tell you everything you need to know about what legal tasks to handle, how much to charge and how to run a profitable business.
$44.95/GSIP

California Incorporator
Attorney Anthony Mancuso
Version 1.0 (good only in CA)
Answer the questions on the screen and this software program will print out the 35-40 pages of documents you need to make your California corporation legal. Comes with a 200-page manual which explains the incorporation process.
IBM PC
(3-1/2 & 5-1/4 disks included)
$129.00/INCI

Nolo's Partnership Maker
Attorney Tony Mancuso &
Michael Radtke
Version 1.0

Nolo's Partnership Maker prepares a legal partnership agreement for doing business in any state. The program can be used by anyone who plans to pool energy, efforts, money or property with others to run a business, share property, produce a profit or undertake any other type of mutual endeavor.

You can select and assemble the standard partnership clauses provided or create your own customized agreement. And the agreement can be updated at any time. Includes on-line legal help screens, glossary and tutorial, and a manual that takes you through the process step-by-step.
IBM PC
(3-1/2 & 5-1/4 disks included)
$129.00/PAGI1

The California Nonprofit Corporation Handbook
(computer edition)
Attorney Anthony Mancuso
Version 1.0 (good only in CA)
This book/software package shows you step-by-step how to form and operate a nonprofit corporation in California. Included on disk are the forms for the Articles, Bylaws and Minutes.
IBM PC 5-1/4 $69.95/ NPI
IBM PC 3-1/2 $69.95/ NP3I
MACINTOSH $69.95/ NPM

How to Form Your Own New York Corporation & How to Form Your Own Texas Corporation
(computer editions)
Attorney Anthony Mancuso
These book/software packages contain the instructions and tax information and forms you need to incorporate a small business and save hundreds of dollars in lawyers' fees. All organizational forms are on disk. Both come with a 250-page manual.
New York 1st Edition
IBM PC 5-1/4 $69.95/ NYCI
IBM PC 3-1/2 $69.95/ NYC3I
MACINTOSH $69.95/ NYCM

Texas 1st Edition
IBM PC 5-1/4 $69.95/ TCI
IBM PC 3-1/2 $69.95/ TC3I
MACINTOSH $69.95/ TCM

Neighbor Law: Fences, Trees, Boundaries & Noise
Attorney Cora Jordan
National 1st Edition
Neighbor Law answers common questions about the subjects that most often trigger disputes between neighbors: fences, trees, boundaries and noise. It explains how to find the law and resolve disputes without a nasty lawsuit.
$14.95/NEI

Dog Law
Attorney Mary Randolph
National 1st Edition
Dog Law is a practical guide to the laws that affect dog owners and their neighbors. You'll find answers to common questions on such topics as biting, barking, veterinarians and more.
$12.95/DOG

Stand Up to the IRS
Attorney Fred Daily
National 1st Edition
Stand Up to the IRS gives detailed stategies on surviving an audit with the minimum amount of damage, appealing an audit decision, going to Tax Court and dealing with IRS collectors. It also discusses filing tax returns when you haven't done so in a while, tax crimes, concerns of small business people and getting help from the IRS ombudsman. This book also includes confidential forms, unavailable to taxpayers, used by the IRS during audits and collection interviewers.
$19.95 / SUIRS

Barbara Kaufman's Consumer Action Guide
Barbara Kaufman
California 1st Edition
This practical handbook is filled with information on hundreds of consumer topics. Barbara Kaufman, the Bay Area's award-winning consumer reporter and producer of KCBS Radio's *Call for Action*, gives consumers access to their legal rights, providing addresses and phone numbers of where to complain when things go wrong, and providing resources if more help is necessary.
$14.95/CAG

Money Troubles: Legal Strategies to Cope With Your Debts

Attorney Robin Leonard
National 1st Edition

Are you behind on your credit card bills or loan payments? If you are, then *Money Troubles* is exactly what you need. It covers everything from knowing what your rights are, and asserting them, to helping you evaluate your individual situation. This practical, straightforward book is for anyone who needs help understanding and dealing with the complex and often scary topic of debts.
$16.95/MT

How To File for Bankruptcy

Attorneys Stephen Elias, Albin Renauer & Robin Leonard
National 3rd Edition

Trying to decide whether or not filing for bankruptcy makes sense? *How to File for Bankruptcy* contains an overview of the process and all the forms plus step-by-step instructions on the procedures to follow.
$24.95/HFB

Simple Contracts for Personal Use

Attorney Stephen Elias & Marcia Stewart
National 2nd Edition

This book contains clearly written legal form contracts to buy and sell property, borrow and lend money, store and lend personal property, release others from personal liability, or pay a contractor to do home repairs. Includes agreements to arrange childcare and other household help.
$16.95/CONT

Divorce & Money

Violet Woodhouse & Victoria Felton-Collins with M.C. Blakeman
National 1st Edition

Divorce & Money explains how to evaluate such major assets as family homes and businesses, investments, pensions, and how to arrive at a division of property that is fair to both sides. Throughout, the book emphasizes the difference between legal reality—how the court evaluates assets, and financial reality—what the assets are really worth.
$19.95/DIMO

The Living Together Kit

Attorneys Toni Ihara & Ralph Warner
National 6th Edition

The Living Together Kit is a detailed guide designed to help the increasing number of unmarried couples living together understand the laws that affect them. Sample agreements and instructions are included.
$17.95/LTK

The Guardianship Book

Lisa Goldoftas & Attorney David Brown
California 1st Edition

The Guardianship Book provides step-by-step instructions and the forms needed to obtain a legal guardianship without a lawyer.
$19.95/GB

A Legal Guide for Lesbian and Gay Couples

Attorneys Hayden Curry & Denis Clifford
National 6th Edition

Laws designed to regulate and protect unmarried couples don't apply to lesbian and gay couples. This book shows you step-by-step how to write a living-together contract, plan for medical emergencies, and plan your estates. Includes forms, sample agreements and lists of both national lesbian and gay legal organizations and AIDS organizations.
$17.95/LG

How to Do Your Own Divorce

Attorney Charles Sherman
(Texas Ed. by Sherman & Simons)
California 17th Edition & Texas 4th Edition

These books contain all the forms and instructions you need to do your own uncontested divorce without a lawyer.
California $18.95/CDIV
Texas $17.95/TDIV

Practical Divorce Solutions

Attorney Charles Sherman
California 2nd Edition

This book is a valuable guide to the emotional aspects of divorce as well as an overview of the legal and financial decisions that must be made.
$12.95/PDS

California Marriage & Divorce Law

Attorneys Ralph Warner, Toni Ihara & Stephen Elias
California 11th Edition

This book explains community property, pre-nuptial contracts, foreign marriages, buying a house, getting a divorce, dividing property, and more.
$19.95/MARR

How to Adopt Your Stepchild in California

Frank Zagone & Attorney Mary Randolph
California 3rd Edition

There are many emotional, financial and legal reasons to adopt a stepchild, but among the most pressing legal reasons is the need to avoid confusion over inheritance or guardianship. This book provides sample forms and step-by-step instructions for completing a simple uncontested adoption by a stepparent.

$19.95/ADOP

29 Reasons Not to Go to Law School

Attorneys Ralph Warner & Toni Ihara
National 3rd Edition

Filled with humor and piercing observations, this book can save you three years, $70,000 and your sanity.

$9.95/29R

Devil's Advocates: The Unnatural History of Lawyers

by Andrew & Jonathan Roth
National 1st Edition

This book is a painless and hilarious education, tracing the legal profession. Careful attention is given to the world's worst lawyers, most preposterous cases and most ludicrous courtroom strategies.

$12.95/DA

Poetic Justice: The Funniest, Meanest Things Ever Said About Lawyers

Edited by Jonathan & Andrew Roth
National 1st Edition

A great gift for anyone in the legal profession who has managed to maintain a sense of humor.

$8.95/PJ

Trademark: How to Name Your Business & Product

Attorneys Kate McGrath and Stephen Elias,
With Trademark Attorney Sarah Shena
National 1st Edition

This is by far the best comprehensive do-it-yourself trademark book designed for small businesses. *Trademark: How to Name Your Business & Product* explains step-by-step how to protect names used to market services and products. Specifically, the book shows how to: choose a name or logo that others can't copy, conduct a trademark search, register a trademark with the U.s. Patent and Trademark Office and protect and maintain the trademark.

$29.95 / TRD

Patent It Yourself

Attorney David Pressman
National 3rd Edition

From the patent search to the actual application, this book covers everything including the use and licensing of patents, successful marketing and how to deal with infringement.

$34.95/PAT

The Inventor's Notebook

Fred Grissom & Attorney David Pressman
National 1st Edition

This book helps you document the process of successful independent inventing by providing forms, instructions, references to relevant areas of patent law, a bibliography of legal and non-legal aids and more.

$19.95/INOT

The Copyright Handbook

Attorney Stephen Fishman
National 1st Edition

Writers, editors, publishers, scholars, educators, librarians and others who work with words all need to know about copyright laws. This book provides forms and step-by-step instructions for protecting all types of written expression under U.S. and international copyright law. It contains detailed reference chapters on such major copyright-related topics as copyright infringement, fair use, works for hire and transfers of copyright ownership.

$24.95/COHA

How to Copyright Software

Attorney M.J. Salone
National 3rd Edition

This book tells you how to register your copyright for maximum protection and discusses who owns a copyright on software developed by more than one person.

$39.95/COPY

The Landlord's Law Book, Vol. 1: Rights & Responsibilities

Attorneys David Brown & Ralph Warner
California 3rd Edition

This book contains information on deposits, leases and rental agreements, inspections (tenants' privacy rights), habitability (rent withholding), ending a tenancy, liability and rent control.

$29.95/LBRT

The Landlord's Law Book, Vol. 2: Evictions

Attorney David Brown
California 3rd Edition

Updated for 1992, this book will show you step-by-step how to go to court and get an eviction for a tenant who won't pay rent—and won't leave. Contains all the tear-out forms and necessary instructions.

$29.95/LBEV

Tenants' Rights

Attorneys Myron Moskovitz &
Ralph Warner
California 11th Edition
This book explains how to handle
your relationship with your landlord
and understand your legal rights
when you find yourself in disagreement. A special section on rent
control cities is included.
$15.95/CTEN

How to Buy a House in California

Attorney Ralph Warner, Ira Serkes
& George Devine
California 2nd Edition
This book shows you how to find a
house, work with a real estate agent,
make an offer and negotiate intell-
igently. Includes information on all
types of mortgages as well as private
financing options.
$19.95/BHCA

For Sale By Owner

George Devine
California 2nd Edition
For Sale By Owner provides essential
information about pricing your
house, marketing it, writing a contract and going through escrow.
$24.95/FSBO

The Deeds Book

Attorney Mary Randolph
California 2nd Edition
If you own real estate, you'll need to
sign a new deed when you transfer
the property or put it in trust as part
of your estate planning. This book
shows you how to find the right kind
of deed, complete the tear-out forms
and record them in the county
recorder's public records.
$15.95/DEED

Homestead Your House

Attorneys Ralph Warner, Charles Sherman
& Toni Ihara
California 8th Edition
This book shows you how to file a
Declaration of Homestead and
includes complete instructions and
tear-out forms.
$9.95/HOME

Elder Care: Choosing & Financing Long-Term Care

Attorney Joseph Matthews
National 1st Edition
This book will guide you in choosing
and paying for long-term care,
alerting you to practical concerns
and explaining laws that may affect
your decisions.
$16.95/ELD

Social Security, Medicare & Pensions

Attorney Joseph Matthews with
Dorothy Matthews Berman
National 5th Edition
This book contains invaluable
guidance through the current maze
of rights and benefits for those 55
and over, including Medicare,
Medicaid and Social Security
retirement and disability benefits
and age discrimination protections.
$15.95/SOA

Legal Research: How To Find and Understand the Law

Attorneys Stephen Elias & Susan Levinkind
National 3rd Edition
A valuable tool on its own or as a
companion to just about every other
Nolo book. This book gives easy-to-
use, step-by-step instructions on how
to find legal information.
$16.95/LRES

Family Law Dictionary

Attorneys Robin Leonard & Stephen Elias
National 2nd Edition
Finally, a legal dictionary that's
written in plain English, not
"legalese"! *The Family Law Dictionary*
is designed to help the nonlawyer
who has a question or problem
involving family law—marriage,
divorce, adoption or living together.
$13.95/FLD

Legal Research Made Easy: A Roadmap Through the Law Library Maze

2-1/2 hr. videotape and 40-page manual
Nolo Press/Legal Star Communications
National 1st Edition
If you're a law student, paralegal or
librarian—or just want to look up
the law for yourself—this video is for
you. University of California law
professor Bob Berring explains how
to use all the basic legal research
tools in your local law library with
an easy-to-follow six-step research
plan and a sense of humor.
$89.95/LRME

NOLO PRESS / 950 PARKER STREET / BERKELEY CA 94710

O R D E R   F O R M

Name

Address (UPS to street address, Priority Mail to P.O. boxes)

Catalog Code	Quantity	Item		Unit price	Total
			Subtotal		
			Sales tax (California residents only)		
			Shipping & handling		
			2nd day UPS		
			TOTAL		

SALES TAX
California residents add your local tax

SHIPPING & HANDLING
$4.00   1 item
$5.00   2-3 items
+$.50   each additional item
Allow 2-3 weeks for delivery

IN A HURRY?
UPS 2nd day delivery is available:
Add $5.00 (contiguous states) or
$8.00 (Alaska & Hawaii) to your regular shipping and handling charges

PRICES SUBJECT TO CHANGE

FOR FASTER SERVICE, USE YOUR CREDIT CARD AND OUR TOLL-FREE NUMBERS:
Monday-Friday, 7 a.m. to 5 p.m. Pacific Time
Order line   1 (800) 992-6656
General Information   1 (510) 549-1976
Fax us your order   1 (800) 645-0895

METHOD OF PAYMENT
☐ Check enclosed   ☐ VISA ☐ Mastercard
☐ Discover Card   ☐ American Express

Account #   Expiration Date

Signature Authorizing

Phone   WM4

NOLO PRESS / 950 PARKER STREET / BERKELEY CA 94710